Praise f

How to Relax in 60

With iPhones, iPads, BlackBerries, and multitasking as staples in our lives, Robert Lawrence Friedman's book could not be more timely and needed. For far too many of us, the two-week vacation in which we took five days to unwind is a thing of the past. What could be more beneficial to our health and well-being than to be able to relax in an instant? That's what Friedman offers us in his new, compelling book, *How to Relax in 60 Seconds or Less*. I highly recommend it.

—James Muyskens, Ph.D.,
President, Queens College,
The City University of New York

How to Relax in 60 Seconds or Less is the book we need on the airplane, in our briefcases, stashed in our desk—better yet *on* our desk. This is a book to read and work with, not just once, but now and next year and the year after. As much as we might like to think we can change the way we live our lives, most of us will notice that we haven't. Life is demanding and we rise to those demands. Learning to do so skillfully, safely, and in a way that does not cave into stress—that is the key to success. Robert is a good guide through the basics of stress reduction and into the uniqueness of stress as each individual knows it. Mine is different than yours. With this book, we get to identify our own patterns of stress and create our own 60-second fixes. What could be better than that? *How to Relax in 60 Seconds or Less* provides a quick fix (many quick fixes, in fact) for a huge problem. Enjoy this book and let it help you enjoy the rest of your life more.

—Dorothy Firman, Ed.D., Co-author,
New York Times best-selling *Chicken Soup for the Mother & Daughter Soul*

Robert Lawrence Friedman is an expert on stress reduction and building resiliency. He has presented many valuable workshops on stress management strategies at our workplace. Though always grounded in research, his strategies are varied, eclectic, and easy to adopt. We have appreciated the insight and guidance he has given our employees.

—Teri Lukin, Director of Health Services
and Work Life Initiatives, Time Inc.

How to Relax in 60 Seconds or Less is ideally suited for our fast-paced lives. It provides an excellent framework for understanding the physiology of stress reactions and offers suggestions for living life in the present—and getting there quickly. Highly recommended.

—Heather MacTavish, Author,
Songs, Science & Spirit

Robert Lawrence Friedman has provided his programs to my students, and he consistently impresses me with his authenticity, clarity, and effectiveness. I've found his stress management techniques to be important tools, and believe that everyone would benefit from them. *How to Relax in 60 Seconds or Less* is an important book for a fast-paced society. We all need it on our bookshelves as a reference tool for living in our stressed world.

—Laurie Mandel, Ed.D., Educator,
Robert Cushman Murphy Junior High
School (New York)

Finally, practical, easy-to-use, and simple but effective methods to reduce your stress! Robert Lawrence Friedman's new book *How to Relax in 60 Seconds or Less* is a must for business people, travelers, parents—just about everyone, since our stress levels continue to rise and will continue to rise. You will learn to identify your "stress signature" and create a "tool chest" arsenal of ways to keep your stress level manageable. This book could save your life.

—Thomas C. Cracovia, Executive Director,
Continuing Professional Education,
Queens College, The City University of
New York

Recently, I was involved with two workshops led by Robert Lawrence Friedman. Robert gave us powerful and useful tools to look at ways to relieve stress and learn to relax in our personal and professional lives. He provided very simple, realistic ways to approach stress, and within a short period of practice we discovered ways to acknowledge stressors, practice relaxation techniques, and find inner balance. The sessions were amazing and life changing. I believe this book offers valuable tools and will inspire readers to take charge of their lives and find new ways to relax quickly and easily.

—Shirley Minter Massey, M.Div., BCC,
Department of Pastoral Care,
University of North Carolina Health Care

"The world is too much with us," the poet William Wordsworth wrote. In this modern world, we are bombarded by stress all the time, but in this illuminating and clearly written book, Robert Lawrence Friedman shows us various innovative relaxation techniques to help us cope with and overcome omnipresent stress. In this fast-paced society, he encourages us to slow down through music, visualization, meditation, etc. He reminds us stress can be dealt with, quickly and effectively, and, to quote another famous poet, Robert Frost. "that has made all the difference."

—Mel Glenn, Author, Speaker, Teacher

How to Relax in 60 Seconds or Less

Robert Lawrence Friedman, MA

ISBN: 978-1-60679-118-9
Library of Congress Control Number: 2010931079
Cover design: Brenden Murphy
Book layout: Studio J Art & Design
Front cover photo: iStockphoto

Healthy Learning
P.O. Box 1828
Monterey, CA 93942
www.healthylearning.com

How to Relax in 60 Seconds or Less

For information on seminars, lectures, and guided imagery tapes that are available, please write or e-mail to:

Stress Solutions, Inc.
66-22 Fleet Street, Suite 3L
Forest Hills, New York 11375
www.stress-solutions.com
rlf@stress-solutions.com

Important

The author has endeavored to be as comprehensive, current, and accurate as possible. Every effort has been and will continue to be made to keep this information updated now and in the future.

Medical Caution

This book should not be used in lieu of sound medical advice. Relaxation techniques can result in changes in physiological processes, including decreases in the level of blood pressure, heart rate, muscle tension, and serum cholesterol. Other physiological parameters may be affected, as well. In addition, if you are using a medication that is designed to affect your body's physiology, the changes you experience may be unduly excessive if you engage in relaxation techniques. For instance, people who are taking high blood pressure medication might find that relaxation techniques lower their blood pressure too much. Accordingly, individuals under medical care or taking medication are advised to get permission from the medical specialist who is supervising their care prior to engaging in the relaxation techniques detailed in this book. More specifically, individuals with heart conditions, epilepsy, hypertension, diabetes, and psychological problems should consult their physician before attempting any of the techniques used in this book

The author and publisher are not liable for loss or damage alleged to be caused directly or indirectly by information contained in this book.

Dedication

I dedicate this book to my wife, Marissa Evangelista-Friedman, my mother, Sylvia Friedman, my brother, Jeffrey Friedman, my sister, Elyse Glenn, my four nephews, Jonathan, Andrew, Sage, and Uriah, and my niece, Sequoia. I dedicate this book to my late father, Philip Friedman.

Acknowledgments

I would like to acknowledge Marissa Evangelista-Friedman, who provided me with much assistance during the editing of this book. I would also like to acknowledge Lynn Levy, whose exhaustive hours reading and editing this script has allowed it to be as finely tuned as it is; Jonathan Glenn for his assistance in editing this book; and Healthy Learning and Dr. James Peterson, for his belief in my projects and my work.

Contents

Introduction

I live in New York City, a town where many people say stress lives. Whether it is the fear of terrorism, the crowded subways, the pressures to succeed, or the cab that wouldn't stop, the list goes on. Of course, New York is not the only town with stress, and it seems there is more stress in our world now than ever before.

I've worn many hats in life, from a stand-up comedian to a psychotherapist to a kindergarten teacher, from a drummer in a band, to a speaker and corporate stress-management trainer.

In each of my careers, I've noticed that different stressors were attached to each job. It seems there isn't a career that isn't laden with some form of stress. As well, outside of our occupations, we have numerous stressors, including dealing with bills and challenges with relationships, from dealing with our families to dealing with our children; we all have stress. Yet, not all of us get sick from stress.

Some individuals who have stressors also have tools, resources, and strategies for dealing with their stress. It is my hope that this book will serve as one resource that you can call upon to provide you with quick methods for dealing with stress.

For some of us, stress is a hidden killer, a time bomb that is ticking away within us as our stressful moments pile up. Ironically, as a society, we have convinced ourselves that stress is a normal part of life, despite the enormity of the problems associated with it. On the whole, it seems that human beings have not fully recognized the deleterious impact stress has on us, or perhaps, we are in denial.

Stress is less about blaming our environment than choosing to take responsibility for our reaction to that environment. In effect, you cannot control the events that surround you, but you can control the way you react to those events.

For the past 16 years, I have trained corporate employees how to relax. Interestingly, what I've found is that most employees want to manage their stress quickly, and then move on to their next busy task.

The primary intention of this book is to inspire you to increase the awareness you have of where you store stress in your body no matter what your career is, to recognize how your thoughts contribute to your stress, and to teach you how to react when you find yourself in a state of stressfulness.

Your Relaxation Tool Chest

Because each of us has different needs regarding stress, one of the goals of this book is to give you a wide range of relaxation techniques, strategies, and tools to have at the ready when life's multitasking chores swirl around you. When you find a method or strategy that works, note it, use it, and keep it with you. Different stress management strategies will work better for certain individuals than others. This book even includes an area for you to create your own techniques based on your experiences in life. If one technique doesn't work well for you, try another. Although this book focuses primarily on using your mind as a vehicle to relax, there are many other ways to relax yourself. Many people prefer exercise as a way to relax, or other active ways such as yoga or Tai Chi. Whatever methods you've tried in the past to relax, it is the basic belief of this writer that you can never have too many relaxation tools in your tool chest. Various questions are asked throughout the book to inspire deeper thought as to what your stress is about as well as methods to help you customize your own stress-relief prescriptions.

This book is about finding an oasis amidst the harried lifestyles many of us have chosen in order to help create a life of greater health. I do encourage you to try as many of these techniques as possible. Be creative and even make up your own.

When you have learned to recognize your stress signature (the way you specifically deal with stress), you will realize that stress does not need to overwhelm you; it can be managed, and in reality, it must be managed or else it will manage you. As triggering events occur, they need not cause the same reaction that they may have caused in the past. It is my hope that you will learn how to catch yourself when you are being triggered by a stressor, and discover that you have the power to retrain yourself toward developing a greater level of relaxation, health, and well-being.

This book has been divided into four sections. Chapter 1 focuses on an introduction to the concept of instant relaxation and the negative ramifications of stress. Chapter 2 focuses on concepts to consider using to help you relax. Chapter 3 has exercises to enable you to create your own stress-relief prescription. Chapter 4 focuses specifically on the techniques which you can use to relax quickly.

Good luck on your journey to relaxation!

1

The Old Way, the Slow Way

Kraig Scarbinsky

When I started writing this book, I wondered if it made sense to write a book about how to relax quickly. At first glance, it seemed to be an oxymoron; isn't there something inherently wrong with relaxing fast? More so, could relaxing quickly actually create stress? "Hurry up, relax" somehow doesn't seem right. Yet, it's what most people are asked to do in today's high-speed world.

Our current world seems to be built on hyperspeed. The old ways of doing things have changed. For instance, what was considered a norm 10 years ago, receiving mail by postal worker, seems quaint and old-school and is even coined "snail mail" as if to mock what was once normal.

Yet, when we do receive a handwritten note or a personal card, many of us would be almost astonished at the amount of time someone must have taken to actually write a letter, put a stamp on it, and then walk to a mailbox.

Certainly, speed is our norm, yet it is in our ability to slow ourselves down that will determine our ability to survive in today's world.

Our Body and Speed

Our bodies are not really built for constant speed. As computer chips do more and more, most of us feel that we, too, must do more and more, whether that means multitasking as computer chips do or watching our emails grow out of control. As the speed of computers increases, so are we asked to increase our speed, until, as with our computers, we may just crash—and many of us do.

Corporate Stress

The American Institute of Stress stated that 90 percent of all adults in America have high levels of stress once or twice a week, and a quarter of all adults are subject to intense stress daily. It was reported that 57 percent of women have stress most of the time.

In many ways, stress is condoned, and most individuals believe stress is an inevitable part of a job. Some have resigned themselves to it, while others have resigned from their jobs to try to eliminate it.

I worked in corporations for over 20 years, and witnessed the toll that stress takes on individuals in our working worlds. It seems that one of the major issues affecting employees is the stress of creating a state of balance in life. Generally speaking, when I teach my course in "Balancing Work, Family, and Self," I have all participants complete an evaluation of their current life balance. In most, if not all, of the cases, when these forms are completed, the bulk of participants state that the majority of their time is spent at work, followed by taking care of others, and then a very small sliver of time is spent focusing on themselves.

It is clear why so many people are burning out. They've forgotten about someone very important.

Why Fast Relaxation?

When my company, Stress Solutions, Inc., provides its stress management programs, the techniques that are most requested by employees are "immediate-need," "I need help right now," "Fix me fast before I lose my job" relaxation techniques, which allow a person to get relaxed and centered quickly, and then get right back to work. We can even call them "triage" stress management techniques, in some respects. The original term for "instant" techniques was "brief" relaxation, coined by Lichstein (1988).

According to Lichstein, in order for a relaxation technique to be defined as "brief" relaxation, the technique needs to be of short enough length that it can be used in any type of circumstance, not be an attention attractor, and provide some degree of relaxation, so that the person can continue doing their task, but in a more relaxed state of mind.

"Deep" and "Brief" Relaxation

Two methods for relaxing are deep and brief. "Deep" often take longer and may have more lasting effects. "Brief" relaxation is an abbreviated version of the longer method.

Brief relaxation techniques generally create immediate results. They are often utilized when an individual is in a tense situation and wants to relax fast. Brief relaxation is often used every day, when stressful experiences demand a quick response: for instance, when you are stuck in traffic and are late for an appointment but don't have 20 minutes to close your eyes, or when you are unexpectedly called into your boss's office and are filled with worry about why your boss wants to see you. It is in those moments when brief relaxation can be most effective.

Why Should You Want to Relax More?

Stress is a pervasive, silent killer. Whether you are aware of it or not, stress is affecting you. As you focus on your life and your success, your career, and your family, just below the surface, stress may be causing damage, either psychologically, physically, or both.

Psychologically, stress has been linked to:

- Difficulty concentrating
- Poor decision-making
- Scattered thinking
- Depression
- Anger
- Worry
- Impatience
- Irritability
- Inappropriate emotional responses
- Loss of appetite
- Overeating
- Restlessness
- Loss of sexual interest
- Increased alcohol and food intake

Physically, stress has been linked to:

- Palpitations of the heart
- Increased blood pressure
- Increased heart rate
- Increased blood coagulation
- Raised glucose levels
- Insomnia
- Muscle tension
- Indigestion
- Constipation
- Diarrhea
- Headache
- Tiredness
- Alzheimer's disease
- Migraine headaches
- Urinary-tract infections
- Heart attacks
- Ulcers
- Cancer
- Strokes
- Aging
- Obesity
- Type 2 diabetes

Clearly, people have many reasons to learn how to manage stress.

Your Relaxation Container

When you are given a container, you fill it. If you need to relax in one minute, you will. If you are stressed, and you realize you are stressed, then you have the freedom to make a choice. The question you need to be asking is: "Do I want to stay stressed?" The latest brain research states that the brain seeks completion. If you say to yourself, "I have only 60 seconds to relax, what do I do?" the brain will seek out the answer. In this case, you need only to turn the page.

2

The Path to Instant Relaxation

Jupiterimages

Intention

I used to do stand-up comedy. My day would begin with one thought: "What is going to be funny about today?" Throughout my day, I would be looking for humorous situations, listening to the words of others, watching and staying focused on where comedy would show up in my life.

It was through having an intention of finding humor that I was able to find it, day in and day out, every single day.

What is your first thought when you awaken? What is your intention as you move through your day? Do you think "I wonder how I will relax myself today" or "I can't wait to breathe deeply today" or "I am so overwhelmed by the amount of things I have to do, I'd rather just stay in bed." In her book, *The Nature of Personal Reality*, Jane Roberts wrote, "You get what you concentrate upon, there is no other main rule." What is it that you are concentrating your attention on? If it isn't what you want, it may be time to create a new intention.

In the appendix, you can start noting the methods, techniques, and strategies that help you to relax. If for some reason one of your tools grows old, try a different one.

The purpose of this book is to provide anyone suffering from stress with a pathway through stress's maze. You are not at the mercy of the stress around you.

21 Days

It takes 21 days to change a habit. Once you have determined those methods that work best for you, the next stage involves incorporating them into your daily routine for at least 21 days continuously. As you continue to include these techniques in your life, you will begin the process of having these strategies become something you do without having to think about it.

I generally recommend taking something familiar that you do every day and then adding a new element to it. For instance, for 21 days tell yourself that every time you open a door, you'll take in a deep breath. Have that as your thought throughout the day. Then as you continue through your day, and open any door, make sure to take in a deep breath. Essentially, you are creating a mental imprint or connection in which you begin to associate turning a doorknob with taking a deep breath.

As you continue to do this practice, you'll start to notice that you are walking into rooms feeling relaxed and not knowing why. It is because you have assimilated this behavior into your routine.

Practice, Practice, Practice

If you want to reduce your stress, you will need to practice the techniques you find here, over and over again, until they become part of your daily routine; until you use them without having to think about it. How long have you been getting stressed in life—most likely, for many years. Part of the process of learning to relax is unlearning some of the ways that you deal with events now. It is a journey.

In Chapter 4 of this book, you will find relaxation techniques, some of which will be easier than others. Build on the ones that are easy for you to do, and then slowly add in others that are more challenging. The more techniques you have in your relaxation tool chest, the better. As relaxing becomes more of a familiar feeling, you will realize that stress is something you can conquer.

Stress is a pervasive, silent killer. Stress is also a cumulative disease. The more you ignore the symptoms of stress, the worse the symptoms will become. The other side is that stress management also has a cumulative effect. Research demonstrates that people who practice stress management literally develop a resistance to stress. In order for you to learn to manage your stress, you will need to deepen the state of awareness you have of your body and your thoughts. What thoughts are you having right now as you think about your stress? What images do you have? Every thought will create an immediate reaction in your body.

How does your body feel right now? Is it tense? Is there a certain part of your body that feels more stressed than another?

How do you know you are stressed?

If you are able to, I'd like to ask you to straighten and tighten one of your arms for about 15 seconds.

Notice if you were breathing when you did the last exercise. Chances are, you probably weren't. In fact, 9 out of 10 people take very short, shallow breaths when they are under stress. When you tighten your arm in this way, you are literally replicating your body's reaction to stress. When you are stressed, your body tightens in the same way as your arm did. If you noticed, you probably didn't realize you weren't breathing until I mentioned it. The body is speaking to us all the time, the question is: do we listen? The short, shallow breath is your body sending you warning level one of stress alert. It is whispering in that moment that you need to *breathe*. Most of the time, we don't breathe in that deep breath that the body is requesting.

If you continue to be stressed, your body will then kick you into stress warning level 2: pain. It is here where you may notice things like headaches, backaches, and shoulder aches. What do you generally do at this stage? Do you look for the reasons behind the pain or take some pain medication? Most of us take pain medication at this stage. But that only masks the symptoms. This statement is very important because it is often much easier to pop a pain pill than it is to unravel the layers of stress that occur in your body.

If you continue to be stressed, the body will then start to yell at you. The body yells at us through immune-system related disorders. The body starts to break down.

Notice the Words You Use

Learning to relax is about cultivating your awareness. As you are walking through your day, notice the words you use. Are they positive words or negative words? Every word you use reflects the types of thoughts you are having. Every negative word will generally create a negative feeling in your body. The positive part of this is that you have control over your words as you cultivate an awareness of them. If you are with your friends and you notice that they are being very negative or complaining, recognize that you don't have to contribute to this climate.

Stress Is Contagious

When someone around you is stressed, you will often get stressed as well. Think about some people in your life who are stressed, and then think about what it feels like to be around them. The good news is that if you are relaxed, that is contagious, too.

The goal is to develop a stress buffer so that when you are near someone who is causing you stress, instead of getting tense, you notice your body's reaction and catch your body before it gets tense. It is a very liberating feeling when you do not get tense around another person. You may even wonder what is wrong that you are not getting tense around them.

You can learn to become aware of when something is stressing you out and then practice doing the opposite. If you know someone who is likely to cause you stress, practice relaxing yourself before seeing that person. As long as you stay conscious of your reaction and monitor it, you should be able to help your body remain relaxed. By changing your behavior and relaxing your body once you notice it getting tense, your body will learn to relax more and more.

Change Your Support Network

Watch the friends you keep around you. Usually, they will reflect your own state of awareness. Developing a network of individuals who bring out your best is important for learning to relax. It is important for your general health to have a network of supportive friends. This doesn't necessarily mean dropping all of your friends, but if your friends are negative, it is a good opportunity to see if they are reflecting who you are. If you are negative, you have the opportunity to learn to be more positive. Some research shows that optimistic, positive people live longer than pessimistic ones. If that's not an incentive, I'm not sure what is.

Mind Chatter

It is important to learn to control the "mind chatter" that exists in our thinking mind, or else it will control us. Deepak Chopra says we have about 60,000 thoughts a day, and out of those 60,000 thoughts, 95 percent of them are the same thoughts we had yesterday, and the day before, and before that, and before that.

Our minds tend to compartmentalize events, so that an event that created stress for you last week will often create the same reaction next week; that is, unless you can change the pattern of thinking through awareness and then through consciously changing your thoughts. Something I do when I find myself in a negative state of mind is to ask myself "What is the most positive thought I can have right now?" That question helps me to redirect my thinking patterns to more positive thoughts.

Awareness of the Present Moment

The present moment is the one we experience when we are fully in the here and now. As you are reading this book, you are probably having many thoughts, swimming through your consciousness. Every thought you have may have a different focus—what will you have for lunch, what do you need to order online, what does your significant other think of you, and so on. Your goal is to stay focused on the present. The benefit of this focus is enormous. Staying present will give you an accurate representation of the moment. It will help your body avoid being locked into some future-oriented fear or past-oriented regret. Because thoughts are associative, once we are in a negative spiral in our thoughts, those thoughts tend to build upon themselves. Another way to think of this is that like thoughts tend to attract like thoughts. Whenever you find yourself thinking of something other than being in the now, your goal is to bring yourself back to the present. Sometimes, people use devices that help them to remain in the present. The breath is used in meditations to bring the person into the present. Another person

I know uses a bell on his leg. As long as he is hearing it, he knows he is present; if it moves into the background of his awareness, he is no longer present.

If you find yourself thinking of something other than right now, bring yourself back to the breath, or find an object that will take you fully into the moment. You may want to continually bring your attention to a part of your body. For example, if your shoulders are tense, relax them. You may want to have a sign available on your desk that reads: "Take a deep breath" or "Drop your shoulders." These signs are a way of reminding yourself to be in the moment.

The more you do these types of exercises, the more you will get to see how your thoughts help to scatter your energies. You may want to devote five minutes a day to simply focusing on your breath, with your eyes open or closed. Remember to be easy and effortless with yourself.

This Moment Is My Power Moment

Sometimes, what occurs in life is that certain belief patterns develop. A subconscious belief may then become ingrained, which then reflects that pattern.

The affirmation "This moment is my power moment" may help you realize that each moment is a new one, and that new positive events may occur.

For instance, a friend of mine believes that it is better to have little excitement about positive events occurring for her. It is her belief that to have excitement about something would open her up to the possibility of being disappointed, which she has been in her life.

For my friend, the present is the power moment may allow her to recognize that because each moment is a new moment, there is as much possibility of something good occurring as something bad.

In my friend's case, she would need to allow for the possibility that there is another way to think other than having low expectations, and would need to recognize that her low expectations may be a self-fulfilling prophecy. The present is the power moment is a very empowering statement because it acknowledges that you don't have to continue repeating the same patterns over and over again, if you choose to face them and change them.

When you repeat the phrase "This moment is my power moment" and begin to believe it, you will start to reclaim the power and belief that you can change your habits and begin to relieve your stress.

Forgiveness

Learning to forgive someone, perhaps even yourself, is a wonderful stress reliever. Learning to find those inner wounds and heal them will help you to create more calmness throughout your day. Otherwise, you may unconsciously attract people into your life that remind you of those individuals that you have to forgive or apologize to, and until you do, you may keep attracting the same unhappy and stressful situations over and over again. Today, write a letter to someone you are angry with but never expressed it. Then, after writing the letter, tear it up, and as you tear it up say aloud, "I release you from my consciousness."

Openness

What shuts you down? What closes your heart? How do you know when you are feeling open? Does your conversation change? When you are open to the universe and trust that everything is as it should be, then you are open to the world. Do you have any friends who are open and others who are generally closed? What is different about them? Sometimes, when we get hurt a lot, our heart shuts down. Your heart being shut down tells you that the world is unsafe and that you need to not let everyone in. Sometimes, this response is healthy, and sometimes it is simply based on a false belief system that the universe is not safe, that you should live in fear, and that it is healthier to remain shut down. Yet, what occurs for many of us is that we are all starving for connection to others, yet afraid to let that starving be known. Our hearts are starved for love, attention, being noticed, and being acknowledged. We need to start opening our hearts with those whom we love and then work our way to those whom we don't know. Have you ever experienced the appreciation of having someone you don't know smile at you? This feeling of connectedness to someone you don't even know can make your entire day feel great. Learning to give to others is one of the key elements of the human race. We need to move from self-centeredness to other-centeredness. Generally, the more you think about the needs of others, the better you will feel about yourself. Questions to ponder: How do I feel around people I trust? Do I generally trust others or fear them?

Ideal Life

Do you remember when you were a child and you had a dream? What was your dream? Your ability to make peace with your present life is one of the keys to having less stress. Having regret about your life is a stressor. For by having regrets, you are saying that you did not do the best you can do. At that moment, you made a choice that you believed was the best. It is very easy in hindsight to say, "I would've been happier if it were this or that way or if I made this decision or that." Let yourself have some inner peace.

Learning to Say No With an Open Heart

One of the challenges many of us have is the ability to say no to someone else. This often occurs when someone is asking something of you, and instead of saying no, you say "yes," while thinking "no." You may have many reasons for finding difficulty saying no to someone. You may have issues of wanting another person's approval. You may have issues of lack of assertiveness. But, generally speaking, when you have a difficult time saying no to others, it will often lead to stress and burnout.

When we say no, we often close our heart. A greater challenge than even saying no to someone is learning how to say no with love and compassion. One of the ways to learn to say no with love is to have empathy for the other person. Many of us are so focused on taking care of others that we forget to take care of ourselves.

When you realize your needs are important, then learning to say no becomes a little easier. When you realize that by saying yes to everyone who asks you for something, you will burn out, the stress becomes a wake-up call to the importance of learning how to say no.

You are important. Your needs are important. Learning to say no with compassion will help you to set your boundaries, and create less stress.

Expansion/Contraction

When you are around friends and family members who are positive and uplifting, you will often find yourself feeling expanded. Friends and family members who berate you and who are critical will often cause a feeling of contraction. It is a contraction of the heart, contraction of the mind, and often contraction of the stomach—and a stress generator. Expansion occurs when you are feeling positive and light. When you are around people who nurture you, you will feel your body relax and your heart soften. As you meet people throughout your day, notice what your body feels like. Sense how your stomach feels when you meet various people today. Each experience, even those that contract you, can change into expanded experiences depending on the way you reframe the event.

Friends

Nurturing friends, hurtful friends, toxic friends, harmless innocuous friends—which ones do you have? Which ones do you have more of? See your friends as your mirror. Do they represent something you are wanting more of in your life in terms of qualities, or do they represent something you are trying to fix?

Your Playful Inner Child

Think about a time when you felt and acted like a playful child. When we allow ourselves to embrace our playfulness, stress is generally released. When we become an adult we sometimes lose the quality of trust and play. My mom taught me the importance of appreciating the small things in life, such as the beauty of nature. What would your life be like if you allowed yourself to rejoice in life's small wonders? When we can cultivate the perception of seeing everything for the first time, providing ourselves with experiences that enable us to experience new things, our life becomes more fun and exciting. Discovering your inner child is about discovering or rediscovering your joyfulness. Without your inner child, you may become locked into the adult mind that has forgotten about the beauty of nature and the joys of life.

Find something that you can do that will help you become a little bit freer. It may be as simple as playing with your children. When we were children, there was no sense of self-consciousness. We were simply in the moment.

3

Your Stress-Relief Prescription

Jupiterimages

Your Self-Contract to Reduce Stress

In order for you to reduce your stress, make a commitment to your success through creating a contract with yourself, and have two people sign it: you and someone else. The purpose of making a self-contract is to make yourself accountable.

Stress is such a subjective experience that unless you make a commitment to someone else, it can be very easy to simply go back to your old stressful ways. The question you need to ask yourself is: "Do I really want to change?"

Contract to Reduce My Stress

I, ____, do hereby promise to
[Your Name]

practice the techniques in this book until they become part of my life. I promise to make this commitment for my psychological and physical health. I do not like being stressed. I do not enjoy the feeling of stress. I have purchased this book because I want to take some positive steps to effect change in my life. I will commit to practicing these exercises over and over again, in both non-stressful and stressful situations. I am important. My needs are important. I deserve to relax now and forever.

____
Signature

____
Witness

Excellent! You have just made a commitment to your success—and the journey begins.

Your Stress Signature

When was the last time you signed your name? Did you ever compare it to anyone else's? Your signature is very unique. Nobody else has a signature quite like yours. The same is true for your stress signature.

When you get stressed, the way your body reacts to stress is unique to you. As well, the specific events that trigger your stress and that cause you to have a stress reaction are also uniquely yours.

The first step to change is awareness, so learning to discover your stress signature is vital to helping reduce your long-term stress. Moving from unconsciousness to awareness will help you change your stress reaction more quickly, for you will start to notice the subtle signs that occur when you are about to get stressed.

For example, what is the first thought you have when you enter a stressful situation? What part of your body gets tense first? When you become aware of what your stress signature is, you can end the stress cycle before it debilitates you. The more awareness you have, the easier and faster you will be able to relax yourself. Every negative or stressful thought would be less stressful if you conjoined it with a relaxing thought. Every tool and resource that you add to your relaxation arsenal will help you relax when you are in stress mode.

When you begin to become aware of when you get stressed, you can then start to develop a battle plan for dealing with your stress.

What happens to you when you are stressed? What is the series of inner processes that occur just prior to the onset of stress and then what do you do about it?

Check what occurs to you when you get stressed.

Your Stress Signature

What happens to you when you get stressed? (Check all that apply.)

- ❑ My shoulders move up.
- ❑ My stomach gets tense.
- ❑ My brow becomes furrowed.
- ❑ I feel fear.
- ❑ My breathing increases.
- ❑ I get sad.
- ❑ My muscles tense.
- ❑ I get angry quickly.
- ❑ I get irritable.
- ❑ I eat junk food.
- ❑ I have catastrophic thoughts.
- ❑ My thoughts race.
- ❑ I have increased blood pressure.
- ❑ I get migraine headaches.
- ❑ I overeat.
- ❑ I get tired frequently.
- ❑ I get restless.
- ❑ I worry a lot.
- ❑ I have difficulty making decisions.
- ❑ I have scattered thinking.
- ❑ I have inappropriate emotional responses.
- ❑ I can't concentrate.
- ❑ I get impatient.
- ❑ I can't sleep.
- ❑ I have a loss of appetite.
- ❑ I drink alcohol more.
- ❑ I lose my sense of humor.
- ❑ I feel helpless.
- ❑ I stop eating.
- ❑ I get headaches.
- ❑ I have a loss of sexual interest

The purpose of the stress signature questionnaire is to determine the physical, mental, and emotional ways that your body gets stressed and the sequence of events that occur when you are stressed. The more aware you are of the process by which you get stressed, the easier it will be to short-circuit the stress reaction. As you notice the process by which you get stressed, your challenge is to use the techniques in Chapter 4 to relax yourself before your body and mind move into more severe stress reactions. Ask yourself, "What are the signs and symptoms that occur when I get stressed?"

Hot Buttons

A hot button usually represents an emotional issue that you have that is often unconscious. If your parents called you "stupid" when you were growing up, and you never resolved the feelings of unworthiness that word generated, when someone else calls you "stupid," whatever their intention, you may have an intense reaction because you never resolved the issue with your parents.

Parents are very good at hitting—and sometimes helping to create—our hot buttons. What are your hot buttons? If you can resolve the hot button through self-examination or with a professional, then no matter what another person says about you, it won't affect you in the same way and with the same intensity of feelings. If your boss says something like "You can't do a job" or "It isn't good enough," that may then touch the part of you that feels unworthy. Sometimes, we compensate for our feelings of self-worth by doing something for someone's approval. Your hot buttons will often create stress when they are pushed, because they represent something that has not yet been resolved. When someone mentions something that touches that hot button, it immediately causes you to get defensive and stressed. Learning to recognize your hot buttons may help you to reduce your stress reaction. When you hear a hot button, practice saying to yourself, "Here is one of my hot buttons. How would I like to react?"

What are your hot buttons?

Your Very First Memory

When working with relaxation, it is important to harness the mind, to develop a positive relationship with your thinking process, and to increase the awareness that you have.

Think about your earliest memory. Where were you? What were you doing? About how old were you? My first memory was of lying in my crib and watching a butterfly mobile turning around.

The reason that I would like you to remember this moment is to start a process of reflecting on the past. Notice how your mind works. Is your first memory a positive one? A negative one?

T. Harv Ecker, international speaker and author of *Secrets of the Millionaire's Mind*, states, "What you do anywhere is what you do everywhere." Notice if your tendency when you think about your past is to focus on negative past events or positive ones.

The challenge you have, then, is to begin to watch your patterns, and when you find those that don't work for you, to change them.

When you describe this memory, bring as many of your senses as you can into the image. The body cannot differentiate imagination from reality. The latest brain research shows that the same brain centers light up whether it is something you visualize or something you experience in that moment. Learning to exercise the mind is important as we focus on using the imagination to create positive images for relaxation. I recommend finding a quiet place to relax. Dim the lights if you find that helps, put on some relaxing music (without words), and then take in some deep breaths. Ask yourself the question: What was my first memory? As thoughts flow in, just note which one feels as if it is the earliest memory, then write it down.

My First Memory

____

____

____

____

____

Your First Relaxing Memory

Now that you've thought of your first memory, think back to your first relaxing memory. What were the elements of that memory? For me, my first relaxing memory was being at Jones Beach in New York with my mom and dad. I recall sitting under a large beach umbrella, watching my father as he placed the blanket on the ground securely.

What are the elements of relaxation for you in your first memory, and how much do those images connect you with other relaxing images?

Learning to connect with those elements that create the feeling of calmness can be very powerful anchors. It is important to develop a tool chest of relaxation techniques. The images in your mind are a good place to start.

If you notice as you are writing that you can't find a relaxing memory, try not to rush the process. Close your eyes and start to move into your past, think about positive images of yesterday, last week, and then slowly move back in time until you come to the very first image that was positive and relaxing. Try not to judge yourself if you can't do it in the first sitting. Most of us don't focus our attention on our very first image of relaxation, so it may take practice. If after a number of tries you still can't find your first relaxing image, then pick one that is more recent.

Write down in this section your very first relaxation image. Write down the elements of the images. Fill in the details.

My First Relaxing Memory

____

____

____

____

____

____

____

Remembering Your Past

Now, let's broaden the previous exercise. Instead of focusing simply on the very first relaxation image you had, let's expand it to include your top five relaxing memories. They can be images of you at any age.

Perhaps you were at a beach with your family or friends. Maybe you went on a cruise somewhere or on a vacation. Think about a moment when you didn't have a care in the world. We can use these moments to recreate that same relaxing feeling. Selective perception is a psychological concept in which, based on the way our mind has been trained, we look for certain elements. Through focusing on your first memories of relaxation, we start the process at the beginning of your life of selectively choosing a random—but significant—memory aligned with the goal of relaxation.

This process is about learning to train the mind to focus on specific images that recreate a positive sensation of relaxation in your body. When left alone, the mind may have a tendency to associate with whatever is predominantly on your mind, be it positive or negative, relaxing or stressful. Making the choice to view those that are most relaxing will help the mind to associate with more of the same. Fill in all the details that you can, in order to begin the process of training the mind to relax when you are needing to relax.

Develop a bank of relaxing memories from childhood: the first time you had ice cream, the first time you played with your friends, your first girlfriend. List five moments in your life when you recall being relaxed.

1. ______________________________

2. ______________________________

3. ______________________________

4. ______________________________

5. ______________________________

How to Use Your Senses to Create Relaxation

Learning to be aware of your sensory experience is very important as it is one of the components of managing stress. The more aware you are of your body, the easier it will be to notice when your body is in stress mode. The earlier you can catch your body in stress mode, the more quickly you will be able to relax. Everyone has a dominant sensory system. Some of us are more comfortable with certain senses than others. For instance, some people are more visually-oriented than aurally-oriented, or more tactically-oriented than visually-oriented. Sometimes, we can give this away by watching how we speak. Do you say, "I can see that" or "I hear you" when you are speaking with someone? If you are primarily an olfactory person, and you try to relax by watching a candle, you may get frustrated at your results. Through honoring yourself, you can relax more quickly.

One of the ways you can use your primary sensory mode to help you with relaxation is to use the mode that works best for you. For instance, if you are primarily a visual person, then listening to relaxing music may not be the best way for you to relax, as opposed to watching relaxing images. If you are an aural person, then watching images may not relax you.

What is your primary sensory mode? Are you a visual person, auditory, oral, or tactile? Once you determine your primary sensory mode, list five ways you can relax yourself.

1. ______________________________

____

2. ______________________________

____

3. ______________________________

____

4. ______________________________

____

5. ______________________________

____

Exercising Your Outer Senses—Visual Awareness

For one minute, with your eyes open, begin scanning an area near you. Breathe in slow breaths, and as you scan the area, notice what you see. Try to scan the area slowly, take in each object, as you take in each object, move deeper within each object so you are not simply looking from one object to the next, but as if you were in deep detail, looking at each object slowly and carefully. As you are doing so, focus your attention inside, and notice what you are thinking. Are you fully present, or are you judging yourself or the exercise?

Once you have focused on your outer sense, close your eyes, and focus on a screen between and above your eyes. Practice seeing those same objects in your mind's eye as if you were actually looking at them. Practice seeing the detail that you just noticed. You may notice that your mind starts to move you in different directions. Your task is to practice refocusing so that you are staying completely centered on the same images you just saw. The goal is to see them as clearly and distinctly as you did the physical images.

Exercising Your Outer Senses—Aural Awareness

For one minute, focus only on what you are hearing. Again, breathe slowly. By slowing down your breath, you change your internal rhythms. Close your eyes, relax your shoulders, take in a deep breath, and begin by focusing on your outer senses. As you breathe, notice what you are listening to. See if you can define the different sounds.

You may notice as you continue to put your full attention on your breathing that different sounds come to your awareness, one after the other. You may also notice that two or more sounds come into your awareness simultaneously.

For this exercise, try not naming the sounds or attempting to figure them out. Simply be aware of the sounds as they change. You may notice that certain sounds trigger certain visual images. Again, let the visual images go, and refocus on your sense of sound.

Focus on a process of imagination in which you recognize that inner senses correspond to the outer senses. Learning to exercise the inner senses is helpful when learning to work with the imagination. When you imagine someone in your past that you had love feelings for, and suddenly you hear a sound you associate with them, that is in your inner sense of sound.

Exercising Your Outer Senses—The Smell of Relaxation

Not only will past memories and images relax you, but smells in your past that you associated with comfort will also relax you. Research has shown that the smells of Pez®, SweeTarts®, and other childhood candy favorites are relaxing. I believe what these findings truly indicate is that scents we remember as a child will often relax us. When you were a child, you probably had little care about the world. Stress was a nonexistent phrase that perhaps you heard your parents talk about, but without the responsibilities of bills and work and dealing with life's tribulations, you didn't have much to be concerned about, generally speaking.

Using our sense memory, we can access moments in our lives when relaxation was simply a part of life. The sense of smell can be a very powerful emotional anchor.

Do you remember some of the smells you experienced as a child, such as the smell of popcorn at the movies? You may have had certain comforting smells in your life. Perhaps during family holidays when there was the powerful combination of love and nurturance and the smells of candied yams and turkey. Or, when your mother or father bought you your first bar of chocolate, and you smelled it and felt their love, a sense memory of love and chocolate and security was born.

Some of the smells I remember that relaxed me were the fresh smell of a potato baking in the oven when I came home from my paperboy route, or the myriad of smells during Thanksgiving, from the stuffing to the turkey, all culminating into one incredible array of heat, aroma, and love.

Think about what kinds of aromas you experienced as a child. Each of you will have a scent prescription for being relaxed. As soon as you smell any of these aromas, you will be transported back in time to a comforting, relaxing, nurturing moment before the gravity of life's responsibilities took their toll on your ability to relax. Write down which scents you remember from your childhood.

____________________	____________________	____________________
____________________	____________________	____________________
____________________	____________________	____________________
____________________	____________________	____________________

Exercising Your Outer Senses— The Taste of Relaxation

Do you remember as you grew up that certain foods relaxed you? The moment you tasted them, you immediately relaxed. It was like a relaxation pill, but it had flavor to it.

Some people describe them as comfort foods. They are different for all of us. Comfort foods reflect the taste of relaxation. They often represent the combination of being loved while being nurtured. Some foods may even have inherent relaxation within them. But let's first focus on those foods that when you eat them, you feel relaxed and nurtured. Were they sweet foods or sour foods, heavy foods or light foods? What were the circumstances when you had them? What are the images that you recall that reminded you of them? Was it a family dinner? Who do you think of when you imagine your foods? If you can visualize the feeling you had anticipating the food being served, then how did it feel when the food first arrived and you first smelled it? What were the combination of aromas that you can recall? What did it feel like when you put the first bite into your mouth, and then you looked around and saw your family or friends? The taste of relaxation may have been immersive. Bring the sensations with you as you recall as many foods as you can that reminded you of the feeling of relaxation and calm. Then, write them down.

Exercising Your Outer Senses— The Touch of Relaxation

Another sensation that may elicit the feeling of relaxation is touch. What does relaxation feel like when you touch it? Does it feel like the soft fur of your pet? Or your hand as it slowly moves over grass, or the feel of a tree when you touch it, or holding your pen when you write?

For me, it was touching the models I put together or the miniature cars. It was the touch of paper when I turned the Archie comic books. Each of us touched something that brought the feeling of calmness to it. Think about what you held that calmed you, relaxed you. Each of these things you touched created an imprint in your brain that when you recall them bring those same feelings back. Was it something soft like a teddy bear? Was it something solid like a locomotive train? Was it something furry like a dog or cat? Visualize all of the feelings you had when you touched your relaxation object. Remember the elements of it. Think about what was around you when you touched them. Did they calm you immediately? Is there anything you can bring into your life now that can remind you of those emotions? Hold something in your hand that creates a feeling of calmness and relaxation for you.

Without allowing the mind to get in the way, just focus on the aspect of touch. It would be best to close your eyes when you do this exercise. Allow your fingers and hands to move around the object. Notice how this feels.

Name five objects that elicit relaxation.

1. ______________________________

2. ______________________________

3. ______________________________

4. ______________________________

5. ______________________________

Exercising Your Outer Senses—
The Images of Relaxation

What images do you associate with relaxation? If you travel back in time, what moments do you recall that relaxed you? At different ages, you may have different images, such as when you and your family played together, when you took vacations with loved ones, when you laughed with friends. Moments in nature, camping, lying on an air mattress—each of us has our own images that when we reflect on them create an immediate "ahh." Certain images may elicit more relaxation than others. Scenes of flowers, your children, family members, your parents—each of these, depending on your relationship with them, your experiences in the past that were associated with them, may elicit very positive relaxing feelings.

Name five images that you consider relaxing. Find ways to add them to any environment that you find stressful. When you are in a moment of stress, focus on the image while breathing slowly.

Regarding nature scenes, some people find forests more relaxing than beaches or flowers more relaxing than trees. Your relaxation quotient is very individual. List five images that relax you when you see them.

1. ______________________________

____

2. ______________________________

____

3. ______________________________

____

4. ______________________________

____

5. ______________________________

____

Portable Relaxation

To build your tool chest, you can recreate relaxing smells, tastes, textures and images in your life by carrying relevant objects (e.g., photographs) with you for those moments when you need a booster shot of relaxation. Using the things you remembered in the previous exercises, write down those that are portable enough for you to carry with you throughout your day to relax you.

Your Favorite Pet

Think about the first pet you had and the very moment you saw that pet. Think about the first time you held your pet, how it felt when your pet showed you love. Think about the smell of your pet, the feeling of your pet when you touched it. Think about moments when you were alone with your pet inside in your home or outside in a park or your yard. Most domesticated pets show their love to us unconditionally; think about how your pet loves or loved you unconditionally. As you reflect on these images, take in a deep breath, see, sense, and feel the emotions you have about your pet.

If you've had another pet at a different point in your life, think about that pet, again focus on the images of this pet, allow yourself to smile. The simple act of smiling relaxes us. Think about the various feelings you had around your pet. Think about their unconditional love, the sounds the pet made to communicate to you. How it felt to hold the pet in your hands or pet them. Visualize the warmth of their skin against your hand. Fill in all the details. Think about a moment when the pet made you laugh or a funny moment when something ironic happened. Breathe it in. Relax into it. Write down a few moments when you enjoyed the loving feelings of your pet.

Being Nurturing

Learning to receive is one of the keys to instant relaxation. The more you nurture yourself, the faster you will relax throughout your day. What have you done in the past that nurtured you? Was it taking a hot bubble bath or getting a shiatsu massage? Was it going for a facial or hanging out with your friends? Your ability to give yourself nurturance will heal the heart and make you whole. If you are a caregiver, it is particularly important to learn to nurture yourself. Once you have written down 20 ways you can nurture yourself quickly, think about how you can include at least one of these in your daily routine. The more you nurture yourself, the faster you will feel relaxed.

List 20 ways that you can nurture yourself.

1. ______________________ 11. ______________________

2. ______________________ 12. ______________________

3. ______________________ 13. ______________________

4. ______________________ 14. ______________________

5. ______________________ 15. ______________________

6. ______________________ 16. ______________________

7. ______________________ 17. ______________________

8. ______________________ 18. ______________________

9. ______________________ 19. ______________________

10. ______________________ 20. ______________________

The Power of Instant Laughter

Laughter is a great method for relaxing quickly. Which movies do you consider the most relaxing? Develop a bank of images that you recall from movies or stand-up comedians that elicit a smile when you think of them. When we smile, we relax.

List your top five comedians and/or scenes from comedy movies.

1. ______________________________

____

____

2. ______________________________

____

____

3. ______________________________

____

____

4. ______________________________

____

____

5. ______________________________

____

____

Take Something Familiar, Add Something New

When you take something you do every day and add a new element, that also helps to ground new behaviors into your body. As an example, tell yourself that every time you open a door, you will take in a deep breath simultaneously. After doing this exercise over and over again, you will develop a new anchor, turning a knob to relax.

Other types of anchors can include driving a car. An example of anchoring relaxation while driving is every time you come to a red light, you take a deep breath in, or every time you make a right turn, you drop your shoulders.

Or, every time you come into your kitchen during the day, do one of the breathing techniques recommended in this book.

Think about things that you do every day. Write down five things that you do every day.

1. ____
2. ____
3. ____
4. ____
5. ____

Next, list five relaxation anchors that you can add to those everyday actions.

1. ____
2. ____
3. ____
4. ____
5. ____

Discovering the Types of Thoughts You Are Having—Stream of Consciousness

Stream of consciousness involves putting either your pen to paper or your fingers to a keyboard, and to keep writing or typing for a certain period of time that you designate. Stream of consciousness exercises enable you to start to pinpoint where your attention is directed. For instance, a friend of mine, who thought he was a very positive person, began doing this exercise and noticed that many of his thoughts were very critical of himself and others. He also noticed, as many do, that when he did this exercise, it helped to release his negative thoughts.

Begin writing down all of your thoughts, without picking your pen up from the paper or your fingers from the computer, for a total of one minute. Notice the patterns.

Self-Sabotage

In order for you to get from where you are to where you want to be, from stress to greater relaxation, you need to know what your blocks to success are. How in the past did you sabotage your success? For instance, did you start something and then, when it was a little difficult, stop? In the past, what has stopped you from making changes in your life? Fill in each of the following sections.

In the past, I have stopped myself from being relaxed through:

____

____

____

____

____

____

____

What positive steps will you take to counter your blocks?

____

____

____

____

____

____

____

Hot Spots

The body has a way of letting us know when we have trouble spots. When you are stressed, your stress will generally travel to one of these hot spots unconsciously, until you become conscious of them through the pain they cause.

Shoulders

Are your shoulders raised as you move through your day? When your shoulders are up, you are doing something called "bracing." Bracing is an unconscious response to stress.

Breathing

We breathe approximately 24,000 times a day. Notice if your breath is shallow or deep. If your breathing is shallow, you are doing thoracic breathing and generally not bringing enough oxygen into your body.

Stomach

If your stress goes to the stomach, your stomach will be tight and tense. Most likely, you will be holding it in throughout your day.

Teeth

If stress goes into your mouth, it will mostly likely show up as gritting or clenching your teeth or having any pain in your jaw.

Forehead

If your stress moves to the forehead, your forehead will probably be furrowed.

What are *your* hot spots?

____

____

____

____

The Importance of Being Positive

Our world seems to place a great emphasis on negativity. We see it on television and radio news. Yet, what we don't realize is that every negative image we feed ourselves with, every negative word we hear from our friends, every complaint that someone has against someone else depletes our resources and sucks our energy. The negative images we see in films can sometimes have a dramatic effect on us.

My mother is a perfect example of this. Since watching the Alfred Hitchcock movie *Psycho* forty years ago, she has not been able to take a shower unless someone is in her house. For forty years, she has visualized the shower scene in her mind and has frightened herself so much to require that someone be present before she takes her shower.

Our mental images help to affect our reaction to the world.

This focus of self-awareness is to explore and notice how much you focus on negativity versus positivity. Your thoughts affect the way you react to the world.

Think of someone you know who is very negative. Next, think of someone positive. What do you notice about how you feel around one or the other?

In order to become optimistic, for one day this week I would like to ask you to not read the newspaper and not listen to the news. The news is so filled with negative stories, murders, anger, fear, and negative information that we have taken these thoughts in and made them our own.

You can train your mind to feel happy, and by creating optimism, you can then create less stress.

Aliveness

Aliveness occurs when you learn to be open to the world and trust that your life is working exactly the way it needs to for you to move to the next step in your growth. Aliveness occurs when you are happy and doing something that really fulfills you. Aliveness occurs when you are in touch with your passion, your life's dream, when you are doing something that you really want to do. When you are doing something other than what you really want to do, oftentimes, you will create a feeling of being shut down, sometimes acting in an introverted way in response to that shutdown.

Most of us need to feel alive. Sometimes, though, when you are at a job that doesn't fulfill you, you may go on autopilot in life. Working in corporations as a trainer, it is easy to spot individuals in this mode. They are usually not very happy, often complain a lot, and feel empty about their life. Every moment in life is an opportunity to regain control of your emotions. Every moment in life is an opportunity for you to say to yourself, "I choose in this moment to be alive, to feel my vitality to live life to the fullest." Remember a time in your life when you felt really alive and vital. Then, write down ways that you can let yourself be and feel more alive.

Inner Peace

We all have experienced inner peace in one way or another. Our ability to find the things that bring us inner peace is a ticket home to deep relaxation and stresslessness. What images come to mind when you think of peacefulness? When have you felt inner peace?

Images and thoughts that create inner peace for me are:

Inner Parents

In our lives, our parents often become internalized. Their messages, ideas, and thoughts become ours, and we either reject them or accept them, consciously or unconsciously. If we accept them, we often do not know where our parents end and we begin. Discovering the messages that your parents gave you as yours and then choosing to keep them or not is very liberating.

What messages did your mother tell you growing up?

____

____

____

____

What messages did your father tell you?

____

____

____

____

Which messages from your parents would help to strengthen you?

____

____

____

____

Don't Compare Yourself to Others

When you compare yourself to others, you forget that you are a unique and special person who has qualities that are uniquely your own. What are your qualities? Write them down and use them every single day as a way to remember who you are. When you are feeling low, take out this list or have a loved one read it to you for one minute. Often, in the world, it is very difficult to let our unique selves out because of fear of ridicule. It is very important that you can find a space, a place to let yourself be free and allow the spontaneous joy within you out. When we compare ourselves to others negatively, we are putting ourselves down, not allowing ourselves to be who we are. The only way to honor yourself is to say, "I am the person I am. I am doing the best I can do in this moment. I release my negative thoughts and allow myself to accept myself as I am."

I appreciate myself because of my qualities.

I appreciate that I am ________________.

I appreciate that I am ________________.

I appreciate that I am ________________.

I appreciate that I am ________________.

I appreciate that I am ________________.

I appreciate that I am ________________.

I appreciate that I am ________________.

I appreciate that I am ________________.

I appreciate that I am ________________.

I appreciate that I am ________________.

I appreciate that I am ________________.

I appreciate that I am ________________.

I appreciate that I am ________________.

Stress as an Opportunity

Many people rationalize their stress away because they may think that everyone has stress. On the other hand, there is a category of individuals who are called "stress hardy." Individuals who are stress hardy have learned to deal with stress by developing an alternate way of thinking about their stress. They view stress as an opportunity and a challenge for personal growth. They believe they have the resources to deal with their stress, and some of the resources they have are techniques for dealing with stress in the moment that it occurs. But to do that, they need to be alert to when they are feeling stressed. People who are stress hardy practice concepts such as learned optimism introduced by Dr. Martin Seligman. Learned optimism is developing a practice of reframing an event that in the past created a negative reaction. Reframing is essentially finding the positive when something negative happens. One of the ways to find a positive in a situation is to ask yourself what it is that you can learn from the situation. The moment you are learning from it, it becomes more positive.

Think about an event that occurred that you felt was negative. Reframing is a muscle so you may want to think in terms of something small that occurred rather than the worst thing that ever happened to you.

Event that occurred to reframe:

____

____

____

The way you will reframe it:

____

____

____

Another way that stress-hardy people view their stressors as opportunities is that they develop gratitude consciousness. At the end of their day, they write a gratitude journal, focusing all of their thoughts on what happened during their day that was positive. By placing their attention on what was positive during their day, they develop a more optimistic viewpoint about life.

Gratitude Training

My father died in 1995. After his death, I thought to myself about how many opportunities I missed spending time with him. Sometimes, unfortunately, it isn't until after someone leaves us that we realize how short and precious time is. We may take for granted what we are given, forgetting how joyful it is to have a father or a mother, until they are no longer with us, and then we feel regret for not having loved them enough or cared for them enough or said to them simply, "I love you." It takes perspective for us to experience gratitude, and yet having gratitude from morning until night for everything that occurs should be the ultimate goal for someone who would like to relieve their stress. Gratitude is a heart opener. Gratitude is the way of being that occurs when we feel grateful every moment for being alive, for being able to breathe, and for being able to feel.

Unfortunately, sometimes it takes looking at another's pain to feel grateful, or looking at a person's disability to realize we should be grateful that we have all of our limbs or are able to see. Think about what you have to be grateful for, and begin writing a list of all the things that you take for granted. When you are feeling stressed or down, take this list out and read it for one minute. It will uplift you, for when we are feeling down, we have already forgotten all of the positives that we have.

Whenever you are stressed, redirect your thinking to what you are grateful for. As you cultivate this technique, you can develop the habit of immediately reframing a negative into a positive, relaxing you instantly.

Write a list of all the things in your life you take for granted and would like to feel more grateful for. Think of all the ways that you don't show love to people you need to. Does everyone in your life know how much you love them? The way you relate to the world directly affects the amount of stress you have in your life. The more positive you are, the more you will find that life events wash over you.

I am grateful for:

____

____

____

____

Cultivating Awareness as a Way to Relax

Everything centers around awareness. Notice what your stomach feels like right now. Is it tight or relaxed? Your shoulders, relaxed or tense? Next, notice what you are thinking about. What did you think about five minutes ago? Did you have a fear, or did you have a thought about an event you were anticipating? When you think, are you typically thinking about positive events or negative events, good expectations or poor expectations? Are you afraid of being laid off? Many of us have hundreds of thoughts every few moments. Yet, each thought will affect you in a way that is either neutral, positive, or negative. If you don't know what kinds of thoughts you are having, then its effect will appear as if it were coming from an unknown source. Yet, that unknown source is not unknown; it is you. We often develop patterns of thinking, often learned. We may have certain events occur in our life that may, if a similar pattern occurs, will then jump to the worst-case scenario, or create a fear of that thing occurring again. If you can realize when you are projecting negatively, you can learn to stop the thoughts that are causing you stress. Most stress occurs not from events, but the way we react to events.

When an event occurs that normally creates stress begin checking how your body feels. What happens when you get stressed? Does your stomach tighten? Do you start to experience a tension headache or neckache? Do your thoughts race? Through awareness, you can learn to change the normal reactions you have to stress. Awareness is the first step to change.

Future Awareness Shifting

When you are feeling relaxed, perhaps when you are on vacation, or feeling at peace in your life, take a moment to close your eyes, and fully feel the feeling, smell the air, hear the sounds.

Learning to control your imagination and becoming aware of when your imagination is creating a negative image is very important.

Learning to recognize when you are in a habit that is negative is important for quick relaxation. When you are feeling stressed, notice the thoughts you are having, and instead of focusing on the negative imagine, imagine the best possible image you can have in that moment.

Learning to harness the power of the mind to focus on the best possible outcomes will relax you because the body cannot differentiate between reality and imagination.

Think about five future thoughts that would make you happy and relax you. When you are stressed, take one minute to focus on these thoughts.

1. ____

2. ____

3. ____

4. ____

5. ____

New Habits

Another element when it comes to creating instant relaxation is the process of retraining your body. What are the habits that you have that are ingrained in your mind that you simply do over and over again because it's what you've always done? What are the thoughts you have that are repetitive but don't serve you. Do you overthink? Do you focus on the negative? Do you focus on what isn't working and ignore what is?

How do you retrain your mind? A quote I read said, "You are as beautiful as your thoughts." Throughout your day, notice any thoughts you are having, and write them down. Learning to cultivate new habits of thinking and acting will help your stress.

Think about one internal habit and one external habit that would help you release stress quickly.

An internal habit could be choosing to think more positively or practicing deep breathing throughout your day. An external habit could be choosing to practice yoga or choosing to exercise more.

Name at least one internal habit and one external habit you would like to cultivate and work on.

Internal Habit

____

____

____

____

External Habit

____

____

____

____

The Reminder

Sometimes, all it takes is a simple reminder to relax quickly. Your body wants to relax. In fact, unless you were about to get hit by a car or chased by a lion, your body is getting damaged by your stress when it occurs chronically.

Stress is an emotional reaction. When you are stressed, you are in your emotions. If you are caught up in your emotions, it is difficult to think about what it is that you need to do to relax.

Occasionally, all it takes is a reminder that you need to do something different from what you are doing, to awaken from the slumber of unconsciousness, a way to take you from your rampant emotions to your rational mind. You can practice specific techniques designed to center you. Some are very simple. One of the suggestions that I provide in my workshops is a simple statement, which can be posted in various places, such as on your mirror, dashboard, desk, and so on. The statement calls forth the action or state of mind that you would like to have in that moment.

For example:

- Breathe!
- Drop your shoulders.
- I am relaxed now.
- I am feeling peaceful and calm.
- This too shall pass. Be here now.
- Smile!

Write down your own statements, then copy them to a 3″ x 5″ card that you can keep with you.

____

____

____

____

____

4

60 Seconds (or Less) Relaxation Techniques

Jupiterimages

Relaxation Through Your Body

The Power of Slow

The ability to relax quickly depends on our ability to slow down—quickly. The more aware we can be of how we do everything quickly, the faster we will be able to relax, for it is your ability to recognize and become aware of your speed, and then slow it down, that will enable you to relax quickly.

We will be focusing on various areas that you can bring your attention to around the nature of speed, for example, walking a little bit slower than you normally do and noticing how that feels, or taking your time the next time you are rushing to get somewhere. People often get into certain rhythms that they may develop out of habit or based on their environment. When you become aware of your typical tempos in life, you may realize that some of them don't serve you.

Try focusing on each of these areas for a week, and then notice how it feels to change the rhythm and tempo of each of them.

Slow Eating

On an emotional level, eating can have enormous ramifications for relaxation. How often do you eat simply to get through eating in order to move to the next task? That's why fast food restaurants were created. When we combine the power of slow with food, we create a food meditation.

Choose something that you *love* to eat, and spend one minute doing the following. Look at it, observe it. If it's in a container or package, hold it, then open it slowly. Look at it, feel it, breathe it in, don't taste it yet. Then, take one bite only, and breathe in as you take this bite. Feel the food as it moves around your mouth, and notice the differences when you chew it. You may notice a complexity to the food that changes as you eat the food.

Learning to practice eating slowly also allows your body to do its job much better. For when you eat slowly and more consciously, you help our stomach do less work. Learning to eat slowly allows you to appreciate the food you are eating more, enabling you to eat with less stress and more consciousness.

Slow Walking

When you focus on doing anything slowly, you create an intention that slows the rest of the body. For one minute, practice slow-motion or meditative walking. It involves cultivating the process of full awareness of what it feels like to walk from lifting the heel, to placing the foot down, to noticing yourself putting your full weight on the foot, and then switching over to the next foot and repeating.

This exercise can be done in many ways. You can do it by having an inner dialogue, following the walking process (lifting heel, dropping foot, etc.) or simply doing it by focusing your attention on the feeling of it. You can then add the element of slow breathing with this, and intentionally slow down your breath as you walk slowly. When you walk slowly, focusing on each step, each instep, and each movement, you become more conscious of how it feels to walk. Walking is not only the means to get from here to there, but also a process for relaxing. Try combining taking a breath with each few steps and synchronizing your breath to your movement. Then, try breathing on every other step, and notice how that feels, then stretch it out so that you are breathing every fourth step and breathing out every eighth step. Notice how that feels.

Slow Talking

For one minute, try talking to someone in slow motion and notice the challenges of it. Begin by talking at your normal rate of speech. Then, incrementally begin to slow down your speech until you are talking in slow motion, as if you were a record player whose plug is suddenly taken out.

As you slow down your speech, deepen your breath and notice how it feels to slow this down. Some people may feel impatient as they stop talking as fast as they had, but others will enjoy and notice that through talking more slowly, they begin to slow down other rhythms as well. Then, change the tempo of your speech, and start to talk very quickly, noticing how that feels. Most likely, talking very quickly will cause you to feel some degree of stress. Sometimes by creating contrasts of speed, you can notice how your rate of speech can both increase and/or diminish your stress levels. Then, very slowly start to slow down and cut the tempo in half, then half again. Notice if you are feeling impatient trying to speak, but stay with it and notice the feelings you have around slowing down. Remember that we develop levels of habituation, where we are so used to speaking in a certain way, or at a certain speed, that when it slows down, it feels uncomfortable. Be with the discomfort. Any time we change something we are used to, it may create some discomfort, but it is also an opportunity for deepening your awareness.

Slow Breathing

Notice how are you breathing at this moment. Whatever the rhythm of your breath in your mind, count it with the following count: one on the in breath, and two on the out breath.

Next, for one minute only, consciously slow down your breathing count so the "one" takes twice as long and the "two" takes twice as long. Extend the one even more as well as the two. As you do this, take deeper and deeper breaths until your breath is moving in slow motion, in and out.

Slow Writing

When we write, we write at a particular speed, but when we write slowly, we are forced to adjust the tempo of our fine motor skills. That can trigger relaxation. Begin now by thinking about something you would like to write. It doesn't have to be about anything in particular. When you write, focus on the speed at which you write each letter, notice that as you slow down your writing, you are also forced to slow down the speed of your thoughts to match the writing. Often, we are speeding up our words that we write in order to keep up with our thoughts, but by slowing the writing down, either we slow down our thoughts, or they all become jumbled in our brain.

For one minute, slow down your hand, slow down the words, slow down writing the letters, and then notice if you've also in the process slowed down your breath. Most likely, you have. You are in the process of retraining your body to work in a slower, more conscious mode.

Body Scan

The body scan is a technique that allows you to recognize where you store stress in your body. Once you are aware of this, you can then release the stress consciously. Though the technique initially takes more than a minute, the goal is to reduce the time to 60 seconds.

Close your eyes, and take in a slow, deep breath. As you breathe in, imagine that you are breathing in relaxation, and as you breathe out, you are breathing out tension. Continue taking long, slow, deep breaths, just noticing the air as it passes through your nostrils and into your body.

The initial goal of the body scan is to adjust your breathing so that you breathe in normally through your nose, but breathe out slowly through your mouth.

Now become aware of your body and how it feels. Notice if you have any tension in your body.

Pay attention to your body sensations. Let's first go to some hot spots. Notice your shoulders and how they feel. Are they up or down? If your shoulders are up, they are doing something called bracing. Bracing is an unconscious response to stress. If your shoulders are up, drop them. This motion sends a signal to your body that you are ready to relax.

Then, notice if your stomach is tense or tight. If it is, relax it.

Next, allow a slight space between your upper and lower lips. Research shows that when the jaws are slightly separated, the body moves into a state of relaxation. The body has various built-in mechanisms to help with stress. We just need to learn how to access them.

Can your forehead relax more? If so, you were tensing those muscles. Allow them to relax. Check your back, neck, stomach, thigh, and calf muscles. Notice if they are contracted or relaxed. If they are tense, relax them.

Take a moment for yourself. Scan your entire body, and notice if you are holding tension anywhere else. Concentrate on letting as many of your muscles relax as possible. Notice how that feels.

Continue relaxing all of your muscles and taking in long, slow, deep breaths. When you are ready, slowly count from 1 to 10. When you reach 10, allow your eyes to open slowly.

The Brief Scan

For 60 seconds, take in a long, slow, deep breath, and then as you release the breath, drop your shoulders. Good. Next, take in another long, slow, deep breath, and this time, soften your stomach completely. Take in one more deep breath, and this time scan any areas in your body that are tense and imagine them relaxing completely. Excellent.

Drop Your Shoulders

When your shoulders are up you are doing something called "bracing." Bracing is an unconscious response to stress. You are stressed, and your body is on alert. When you drop the shoulders, you send a message to your body. The message is "It's okay to relax," and then occasionally you'll also find yourself taking in a deep breath.

One way to relax instantly is to notice the way your body tenses, and then practice reversing what the body does. The practice of unbracing is a very powerful technique for creating instant relaxation.

As you walk through your day, notice if you are unconsciously holding tension in your shoulders. The force of gravity will drop your shoulders when you do not resist gravity. Throughout your day, allow the force of gravity to bring your shoulders down. Often, your shoulders will be up because they are expecting the next stressful moment to occur.

The shoulders may also metaphorically represent shouldering responsibility or taking on burdens. The simple act of dropping your shoulders will not only feel good, but will send a message to your mind that it is time to relax.

Right now, notice if your shoulders are up. If they are, drop them. Let them all the way down. Learning to catch those areas where there is stress is important for managing your stress and learning to instantly relax.

Occasionally, the shoulders are up very subtly so even if they don't appear to be, take a deep breath in and then as you exhale let the shoulders drop even more.

Once they drop, try helping them drop more.

The next stage of this exercise is to then notice when they try to raise up throughout your day, and catch your shoulders before they brace.

Desk Massage

When you are at your desk, for one minute give yourself the massage that you would like others to give you. Shrug your shoulders upward. Then, drop your shoulders. Using your right hand, massage your left shoulder. With your left hand, massage your right shoulder. Knead your thumb, and find any spots that are painful. Rub them gently. Stretch your arms, your legs. Take in a deep breath, and come back into the present.

The Power of Smiling

It seems our body has built into it moments in our lives when we were happy, and when we smile—even if we don't truly feel it—we can access those emotions. Dr. Israel Weyenbaum did research in which he put pencils in students' mouths (horizontally). He found that when the students' mouths were forced to smile because of gripping the pencil in their mouths (creating a fake smile), they had happier thoughts. Smiling sends an opposite message to your body to relax. When you are stressed, do the opposite, and smile.

The Power of Love

For 60 seconds, focus your attention on someone you love or have loved. See that person's face, and imagine the feelings you had when you were with that person. Smell the smells of the person. Bring all of it into focus, and relax.

A Deep Breath

When you take in a deep breath, you trigger the body's natural relaxation response. Numerous researchers found that the deep breath, although very simple, also is very effective for triggering the body's relaxation. Begin this technique by noticing how deeply you can take a breath. As you take the breath, notice how far into the diaphragm you can breathe. The more you can expand the breath into the diaphragm, the more effective your relaxation will be. Practice each day making your breath a bit deeper so that your diaphragm expands more and more with each breath.

An Exhalation

Research has also demonstrated the importance of breathing out to relax. For one minute, practice taking a deep breath in and then an even slower breath out. Notice how it feels to breathe out very, very slowly. Do this for a few moments and notice the changes in your body.

Relaxation Through Sight and Sound

The Power of Sight

Watch a Candle

Focus all of your attention on a burning candle for one minute. As you focus on the flame, see the fire burning away all of your stress. Let the flame awaken in you your own light and the positive energy within you. Use the flickering flame to create a sensation of relaxation and ease. Breathe slowly and deeply as you visualize yourself becoming the candle.

Traffic Light

As traffic lights typically change quickly, they can be great quick stress relievers! When you stop for a traffic light, focus your attention on the red light completely. Take as many slow deep breaths as you can until the light turns green.

The Power of Sound

Relaxation and Music

For one minute, focus your full attention on music that relaxes you. Try to keep your attention completely focused on the sounds. When you listen to music that inspires you, it is often an immediate stress reliever. The problem is that when you are stressed, you are probably not thinking about what type of music to listen to. Choose music that calms you. Some suggestions include Deuter, Kitaro, and Liquid Mind.

Rhythms of the Drum

A drum is a very powerful way of releasing inner tensions and stress. When you hit a drum, its best to use a hand drum. Focus on anything that is causing you stress. It seems that the drum allows an individual to go from emotion to release, without needing to find the right words. The drum puts you squarely into the here and now; it will empower you, and it will provide a vehicle for releasing your stress. For one minute, hit a drum, focusing on releasing your stress through it.

The Power of Free Dance

When you dance to music in a way that is improvisational and free, it allows the body to release any tension and tightness within it. Dance for one minute, focusing solely on letting go of the mores of good dancing. In one of my programs on inner freedom, I have my participants dance as if they were on an alien planet. Try it.

Relaxing Affirmations

Practicing self-talk is a wonderful way to relax. For one minute, focus on and repeat words that relax you. Often when we give ourselves the suggestion to simply relax, we experience it as if it were happening at that moment. What words could you say to yourself that would relax you right now?

Listening to Silence

Close your eyes, and spend a minute focusing your attention not on the sounds around you, but rather the silence between the sounds. See if you can direct your attention to the spaciousness of the silence. Breathe into the silence. After one minute, open your eyes.

Relaxation Through Guided Imagery

Guided Visualization

Learning to harness the imagination can be a very powerful force for your relaxation. It is important to learn to catch yourself when you are focusing your attention on negative images. For if it is an imagery of danger, your body is most likely perceiving that the danger is actually occurring and will create a stressful reaction in your body.

Guided imagery exercises are best done with your eyes closed, so make sure you are not driving or doing anything that requires your eyesight. Once the process is complete, open your eyes, and notice how you are feeling. Each imagery exercise is designed to take one minute or less.

The following guided visualizations are intended to provide you with positive mental imagery in order to learn to relax yourself when you are tense or tight.

Your imagination is, in a sense, a muscle. The more you practice using it, the better your results.

Guided Imagery Practice Skills

Close your eyes. Take in a deep breath, and focus solely on the inner blackness with your eyes closed. It is a good practice, learning to open your inner senses. Visualize what it would feel like if you could flick a switch, and instead of focusing externally, you could focus internally instead.

The inner senses, as with the outer ones, are sight, sound, smell, touch, and taste. In all the following exercises, practice for only one minute.

Let's begin with focusing on sight. Practice imagining colors. They can be simply dots or large circles or the entire landscape in front of you as a color. See how long you can place your attention on the color before you have a thought that takes you away from the exercise.

Practice imagining sounds. Imagine the sound of an ice cream truck when you were a child. Imagine the sound of an orchestra. Imagine the sound of someone laughing.

Practice imagining smells. Imagine the smell of an apple after you have first cut it open. Imagine the smell of a beautiful rose. Imagine the smell of pine.

Practice imagining the use of touch. Imagine yourself touching a tree. Imagine yourself petting a dog. Imagine yourself touching cool water.

Practice imagining your taste. Imagine the taste of the apple you smelled before, imagine the first bite and then subsequent bits. Imagine the taste of your favorite candy and when you first put it into your mouth. Imagine the taste of your favorite food.

We will now practice various visualization exercises to help continue your journey into relaxation using the imagination. Except as noted, these imagery techniques can be completed in 60 seconds or less.

The Dial

Begin by taking in a long, slow, deep breath. In your mind's eye, focus on a dial set to 10, which represents the level of tension you have in your body at that moment.

In your imagination, see the dial, moving to nine. As it moves, you may notice that you feel a little bit less stressed. Move the dial to eight, and the tension becomes a little less. Moving it to seven, then six, then five. You are noticing a significant improvement in your tension.

Moving it to four, three, two, one, you may notice that your tension is feeling considerably better and is down to zero. Your tension has dissipated. You are in control of the level of tightness in your body. Do this technique continuously throughout your day.

Electrical Switches

Note: Although this technique will initially take longer than one minute, the goal is to practice until you can complete it within 60 seconds.

Close your eyes, and allow yourself to breath naturally. Take in a slow deep breath, and with each breath allow yourself to relax more and more. In just a few seconds, imagine that imaginary electrical switches are placed throughout your body. Each switch effects the tension in various parts of your body. First, I would like you to become aware of where the switches are.

Imagine an electrical switch on your left foot that controls all the tension in your left foot; a switch on your right foot that controls all feelings in the right foot; a switch on the top of your left leg just below the hip that controls all muscles and feelings below the left leg, including the leg muscles, feet, and toes; an electrical switch on the right leg just below the hip that controls all tension in the leg muscles, feet, and toes. You have a switch on your right shoulder that controls the right arm, biceps, triceps, hand and fingers, and right shoulder. You have a switch on your stomach, a switch on your lower spine, middle spine, and upper spine. You have an electrical switch on the top of the head, which controls all facial muscles. The master switch is in the back of the neck with a dimmer just below that.

Practice turning the switches off. As each switch is turned off, visualize that part of the body becoming totally and completely relaxed. Then, practice turning the switches on, but notice that you can control the level of stress by adjusting the master switch in the back of your neck. Practice recognizing your ability to create relaxation in your body when you need to feel it.

Red Traffic Light

Close your eyes.

Imagine you are driving your car, and you are stopped at a red light. Put all of your attention on the red circle of light. View the redness of the light as a reflection of the current level of stress in your body.

Imagine that the red light turned yellow. As the red light turns to yellow, imagine that your stress levels immediately diminish by 50 percent.

Imagine that the yellow light turns green. As the yellow light turns green, visualize all of your stress washing away.

Open your eyes.

The Helium Balloon

Close your eyes.

Visualize yourself as a colorful balloon. Imagine that next to you is a canister of helium. Imagine yourself filling up with the helium. As the helium continues to fill you up, you begin to feel lighter and lighter. Imagine that the lightness of the helium is replacing the stress in your body. As this continues to happen, you begin to float higher and higher, relaxed and light.

See yourself in your imagination floating higher and higher in the air. As you begin to lift, feel all of your stress and cares floating away. Feel yourself breathing deeper and deeper, and as your breath deepens imagine yourself getting lighter and lighter.

Allow yourself to feel calm, centered, and relaxed.

Open your eyes.

Inner Flight

Close your eyes.

Imagine yourself on a beautiful beach. It might be a beach you're familiar with, or one you've never seen before.

Imagine that you can open your inner senses of sight, sound, smell, touch, and taste—the same senses that correspond to your outer ones.

On this beach, see a seagull in front of you. Because you are in the imagination, change places with the seagull so that you are the seagull, and the seagull is you. Notice how you look through the eyes of a seagull.

For one minute, imagine yourself flying above the clouds, gliding as you fly higher and higher. From the perspective of this height, let everything go except the enjoyment of being this bird in flight. Finally, see yourself gliding down to the beach, until you see yourself on the beach.

Change places with yourself, so that you are now the bird, and the bird is now you. How did it feel becoming this bird? Notice how you are feeling having come back into your body. Open up your outer senses, sight, sound, smell, touch, and taste.

Open your eyes.

The Air Mattress

Close your eyes. Take in a deep breath.

In your mind's eye, see a pool of warm water. It is very inviting. You are very safe. In the water is a fully blown up air mattress, floating back and forth. Now, see yourself getting on the air mattress. Feel the warmth of the air mattress as it has been lying in the sun.

Imagine yourself lying down on the air mattress. You are completely supported by the water. The air mattress and you are gently floating back and forth in synch with the waves.

Put your hand into the water, and feel the warmth of the water against your hand. Feel the warmth of the sun against your back and the cool breeze against your forehead.

See yourself getting off the air mattress and stepping back onto the side of the pool. Enjoy the sensations of relaxation throughout the rest of your day.

Open your eyes.

Floating Sensation

Close your eyes.

Learning to develop the sensation of floating is a wonderful stress reliever. The key to floating is to let all muscular tensions go and to let all thoughts be released. Focus on the sensation of lightness. In this case, imagine what it would feel like to be floating over your bed. Imagine the feeling of lightness all around you. Imagine the feeling of not having a care in your mind.

Open your eyes.

Your Inner Sanctuary

Amidst the dramas of life, it is important to have an inner sanctuary where you can relax and let go. When you have one place that you visualize consistently all the time, it becomes an anchor of relaxation.

Close your eyes, and imagine what the most ideal, beautiful haven of relaxation would be for you. It could be a place you've been to, or one that you've only imagined. It could be a forest, or a beach, or a place you went on vacation. It could be a place you went alone or one you went to with your family.

I'd like you to fill in all the details: how it felt like to be there, the smells you imagine, the images you would see, the sounds you would hear, the elements you would touch, or any tastes you could imagine. Imagine what it would be like to be in this space and you have absolutely nothing that you have to do.

This is your sanctuary, a place where you go when you need to completely let go of everything and anything that is keeping you from being relaxed. Continue to visit this inner sanctuary when you are feeling the need to separate from the dramas of your life.

Open your eyes.

The Box

Close your eyes, and take in a deep breath.

One of the resources that can be very helpful for relaxing is to create an imaginary box that would allow you to release and let go of anything that is happening in your life that is causing your stress. The box serves as a metaphor of release and safety.

In your mind's eye, see a box that is empty. In creating the box, adorn it in any symbols of relaxation and strength that feel appropriate.

Imagine that you are putting into this box the symbols of anything and everything that is causing you stress. See each object released from you and then placed into the box. As you let each thing go, feel yourself getting lighter and lighter.

Open your eyes.

The Protective Shirt/Top

As some superheroes have a protective outfit that enables them to become greater than they are, a helpful exercise for relaxation is to imagine yourself wearing a garment that immediately triggers relaxation. You can also create this in reality.

Close your eyes.

Imagine yourself walking to a clothes closet that has only one beautiful top/shirt. As you glance at this shirt/top, you know that when you put it on, it will immediately release your stress and tension, without effort or strain. It will be an immediate release.

Walk up to this shirt/top, and take it off the hanger. Just touching the shirt/top creates a mild feeling of relaxation.

Imagine yourself putting your right arm through the sleeve, and then putting the left arm through the sleeve. As if it had very magical properties as you put this shirt on and straighten it, it relieves you of all stressful feelings. Button each button, and as you do, notice the feeling of protection and relaxation deepens.

Open your eyes.

Inner Senses and Relaxation

As described previously, your inner senses correspond to your outer senses. Your imagination is like a muscle—the more you practice using it, the clearer the visualizations will become. The goal with these next series of visualizations is to focus on using your inner senses to imagine specific relaxing images.

Visualizing the Scents of Relaxation

Scents from your past that you associated with comfort will relax you. When you were a child, you likely had few cares about the world. Stress was a nonexistent word, or perhaps you heard your parents talk about it. However, without the responsibilities of adulthood, you probably didn't have much to be concerned about.

Close your eyes, and make believe you can smell the scents you wrote down in Chapter 3 right now. Breathe them in, visualize them clearly. Allow yourself to become immersed in the scents. Open your eyes after 60 seconds.

- Breathing in Your Favorite Flower

Close your eyes and imagine your favorite flower in front of you. See all the details. Now imagine yourself bringing the flower closer to your face and right up to your nose. As you can just about feel the petals of the flower tickling your nostrils, take a long, slow, deep breath in and imagine yourself breathing in the beautiful scent of this flower. Open your eyes after 60 seconds.

Visualizing the Sounds of Relaxation

With your eyes closed, begin to think about the sounds that you wrote down in Chapter 3. For some it may be the sound of the ebb and flow of the ocean, for others the sounds of crickets. Imagine that you are listening to those sounds now. As you listen to the sounds, practice focusing all of your attention on them so that your focus is on these calming relaxing sounds more than on any sounds you are listening to from the outside.

- Hearing the Ebb and Flow of the Ocean

Imagine yourself at your favorite beach. Feel the warmth of the sand below your feet. Feel the sun against your back. Imagine yourself lying down on your favorite blanket and as you relax deeper and deeper, imagine the sounds of the ocean as the waves ebb and flow in a slow rhythmic pace. You may even want to begin to breathe in a pattern that reflects this rhythm. Open your eyes after 60 seconds.

Visualizing the Sights of Relaxation

Sights from your past that you associated with comfort will relax you. What objects, people, animals, and natural elements relax you immediately when you see them? Sometimes, the relaxation comes due to a positive association. In other cases, it is more of a natural innate relaxation that occurs, for instance when you view a beautiful rainbow or a majestic mountain. Close your eyes and visualize the sights that you wrote down in Chapter 3. Allow your mind to free associate the people, animals, and natural elements that have created a feeling of calmness and ease in you when you've seen them.

• Light From Bright to Dim

Visualize a light that is very bright in your mind's eye. Visualize that at the same time you can see a dimmer switch. Imagine yourself turning the dimmer switch counterclockwise, and as you slowly turn the dimmer switch, the light begins to get dimmer and dimmer. As the light gets dimmer, imagine your stress becoming less and less. As it dims, you relax more and more.

Visualizing the Touch of Relaxation

Certain objects elicit a feeling of calmness when we touch them. For some people, it is the feeling of a mattress as you're about to get into bed to sleep. For others, it may be the feeling of touching the fur of your pet. It may be the feeling of touching a natural element such as tips of grass. Close your eyes and visualize yourself touching the things you wrote down in Chapter 3 that create a feeling of relaxation in you.

• Pets You've Loved

Imagine moments in your life when you had a pet that you loved or love. See the pet in your mind's eye. See the pet's personality, and imagine how it feels to touch the pet and hold the pet. See moments when the pet would lay in bed with you. See moments when the pet would visit you in troubled times. Most pets have an innate sense of when their owner is in need. Imagine a moment when your pet came to your aid.

Visualizing the Tastes of Relaxation

Tastes that you associate with comfort will relax you. Think about when you were a child, and you ate your favorite food. For some, it is candy, for others it is a meal associated with a holiday or festive occasion. For others, it is a meal your mom prepared for you when you weren't feeling well. Allow yourself to visualize and taste those foods that you wrote down in Chapter 3. Imagine yourself slowly picking up the food or the utensil and then putting the food into your mouth, then imagine the nuance of flavors calming and relaxing you.

• Drinking the Relaxation Elixir

Close your eyes and imagine that you are about to drink an elixir that will absolutely and totally relax you. As you anticipate drinking this liquid, know that the moment it touches your lips, your entire body will go limp and relax. Open your eyes. Try this exercise with real purified water.

Combining All Senses

With your eyes closed, take a deep breath in. For one minute, focus on your senses of sight, sound, smell, touch, and taste. Begin with the sensation of smell. Notice what you are smelling in this moment. Bring in the sensation of sight. With your eyes closed, see something simple. Bring in the sensation of touch, and then the sensation of hearing. Finally, imagine yourself tasting something that you associate with relaxation. Practice bringing all your senses in together as if they were a symphony playing one song. Open your eyes.

Imagining Nature

Close your eyes. Visualize a scene in nature that you witnessed in your life. It could be any scene. Fill in the details. Smell the air, touch the objects around you. See the details clearly. Open your eyes.

Becoming the Wind

Close your eyes. The wind goes with the flow. As the air current moves the wind, it moves without thought of right or wrong. Imagine yourself as the wind moving, with the airstream. Nothing to do, nowhere to go. Open your eyes.

Becoming a Tree

Close your eyes. Visualize yourself as a tree, rooted to the earth, grounded. See your branches and leaves floating and rustling with the wind. Feel the effortlessness of it. Open your eyes.

Becoming an Ocean Current

Close your eyes. Imagine yourself as an ocean current, moving with the wind, floating, no thought, except that which you are directed. Open your eyes.

Becoming an Ocean Wave

Close your eyes. Visualize yourself as an ocean wave. See yourself moving back and forth, ebbing slowly to and fro. The ocean wave can be seen as a metaphor for the breath. As the breath moves in and out, the ocean wave reflects that motion. Opening your inner senses, see, sense, and feel the ocean wave as you. Smell the ocean around you. Taste the salt of the water that you are. Feel the stillness of the ocean below you. Open your eyes.

Becoming a Leaf

Close your eyes. Imagine yourself shrinking to the size of a leaf. How would it feel to be a leaf? Imagine yourself floating in the sky as a leaf. Open your eyes.

The Past

Close your eyes. Focus all of your attention on an incredible moment in your past, any moment. Then, bring it all into focus as if it were happening again in the moment you are thinking about it. Breathe into the mind, and see, sense, and feel it. Open your eyes.

The Future

Close your eyes. Focus all of your attention on your most ideal future. Picture it as right now, as if you were suddenly transported into that moment. After one minute, release it. Open your eyes.

Strands of Consciousness

Close your eyes.

Visualize strings from your solar plexus, which represent strands of consciousness that extend from you to anyone else in your life that is creating a feeling of stress in you.

See yourself pulling out and detaching each of these strands as if they were attached with fishhooks.

As each strand detaches, feel yourself becoming lighter and lighter and more and more released from your stress. Letting go of the strands is a symbolic way of letting go of issues you may have with another person.

Open your eyes.

Probable Event

Close your eyes. Focus on a stressful experience that happened during your day, and then imagine another choice that you could have made that would have created a more relaxed feeling. Open your eyes.

Conclusion

Throughout this book, I have offered you various tools for practicing quick relaxation. As you practice these tools and strategies, write down the methods that work best for you in the form provided in the appendix.

Good luck with staying relaxed!

Appendix: Your Stress Prescription

The Methods That Work Best for Me

- ____________________
- ____________________
- ____________________
- ____________________
- ____________________
- ____________________
- ____________________
- ____________________
- ____________________
- ____________________
- ____________________
- ____________________
- ____________________
- ____________________
- ____________________
- ____________________

The Methods That Work Best for Me

- ____
- ____
- ____
- ____
- ____
- ____
- ____
- ____
- ____
- ____
- ____
- ____
- ____
- ____
- ____
- ____
- ____
- ____
- ____
- ____

The Methods That Work Best for Me

- ____
- ____
- ____
- ____
- ____
- ____
- ____
- ____
- ____
- ____
- ____
- ____
- ____
- ____
- ____
- ____
- ____
- ____
- ____
- ____

Recommended Products

DVDs

The following DVDs by Robert L. Friedman and Healthy Learning are available at his website (www.stress-solutions.com):

Balancing Work, Family, and Self
Being the Best You Can Be and Staying Motivated
Creating Your Best Life Now
Drumming and Wellness for Adults
Drumming and Wellness for Children
Humor as a Tool for Good Health
Managing Stress
Occupational Stress: Understanding the Basics
Psychology of Weight Loss
Relaxation Techniques: Relax Now

Online Courses

The following interactive online stress management courses are available at Robert L. Friedman's website www.stress-solutions.com:

Managing Work-Related Stress
Balancing Work, Family, and Self
Humor and Optimism as Tools for Good Health
Conflicts, Relationships, and Stress
Communication Skills: Adjustment

Music

Deuter. *Buddha Nature*
Deuter. *Earth Blue*
Friedman, Robert. *Inner Flight*
Halpern, Steven. *Effortless Relaxation*
Halpern, Steven. *Letting Go of Stress*
Halpern, Steven. *Tonal Alchemy*
Halpern, Steven. *Music for Sound Healing*
Kitaro. *Silk Road, Volumes 1 and 2*
Kitaro. *The Kitaro Essential*
Liquid Mind. *Slow World*
Liquid Mind. *Liquid Mind III: Balance*
Liquid Mind. *Liquid Mind IV: Unity*
Liquid Mind. *Liquid Mind V: Serenity*

Technology

The emWave Personal Stress Reliever is a stress relief technology designed to help you balance your emotions, mind, and body. This scientifically validated, handheld stress reliever was developed by the Institute of HeartMath (IHM).

The Biofeedback Stress Relief Coach is a biofeedback device that provides relief for stress in as little as 15 minutes without the use of medication by teaching you to synchronize your breathing with the activity of your nervous system activity for optimal physical and mental relaxation.

Online Resources for Stress

www.dissolvestressnow.com (relaxation software)
www.heartmath.com (relaxation software)
www.thesharm.com (self-hypnosis and relaxation machine)
www.instant-relaxation.com (relaxation software)
www.mypersonaloasis.com (online relaxation software)
www.stress.org (American Institute of Stress)
www.stress-solutions.com (training programs for stress management)
www.softplatz.com (relaxation software)

References

Alpher, V.S. & Blanton, R.L. (1991). Motivational processes and behavioral inhibitions in breath holding. *The Journal of Psychology,* 125(1):71-81.

Benson, H. (1984). *Beyond the Relaxation Response.* New York: Times Books.

Benson, H. (1983). The relaxation response: its subjective and objective historical precedents and physiology. *Trends in Neurosciences*, 6:281-284.

Benson, H. & Klipper, M. (1976). *The Relaxation Response*. New York: Avon.

Cohen, S., Tyrrell, D.A.J., & Smith, A.P. (1991). Psychological stress and susceptibility to the common cold. *New England Journal of Medicine*, 325:606-612.

Cohen, S. & Williamson, G.M. (1991). Stress and infectious disease in humans. *Psychological Bulletin*, 109:5-24.

Friedman M. & Rosenman R.H. (1974). *Type A Behavior and Your Heart.* New York: Kroft.

Lazarus, A.A. & Mayne, T.J. (1990). Relaxation: Some limitations, side effects, and proposed solutions. *Psychotherapy: Theory, Research, Practice, Training*, 27(2):261-266.

Kabat-Zinn, J. (1993). Mindfulness meditation: Health benefits of an ancient Buddhist practice. In Goleman, D. & Gurin, J. (Eds.). *Mind/Body Medicine*. Yonkers, NY: Consumer Reports Books.

Kiecolt-Glaser, J.K., Glaser, R., Strain, E.C., Stout, J.C., Tarr, K.L., Holliday, J.E., & Speicher, C.E. (1986). Modulations of cellular immunity in medical students. *Journal of Behavioral Medicine*, 9:5-21.

Kiecolt-Glaser, J.K. & Glaser, R. (1991). Stress and the immune system: human studies. In Tasman, A. & Riba, M.B. (Eds.) *Annual Review of Psychiatry*, 11:169-180. Washington, D.C.: American Psychiatric Press.

Lehrer, P.M., Hochron, S.M., McCann, B., Swartzman, L., & Reba, P. (1986). Relaxation decreases large-airway but not small-airway asthma. *Journal of Psychosomatic Research*, 30:13-25.

Lenderking, W. & Santorelli, S.F. (1992). Effectiveness of a meditation-based stress reduction program in the treatment of anxiety disorders. *American Journal of Psychiatry*, 149:936-943.

LeShan, L. (1974). *How to Meditate*. New York: Bantam.

Lichstein, K.L. (1988). *Clinical Relaxation Strategies*. New York: John Wiley.

Looker, T. & Gregson, O. (1989). *Stresswise: A Practical Guide for Dealing With Stress.* London: Hoder and Stoughton,

Lum, L.C. (1977). Breathing exercises in the treatment of hyperventilation and chronic anxiety states. *The Chest, Heart, and Stroke Journal*, 2:6-11.

Lynn, S.J. & Rhue, J.W. (1977). Hypnosis, imagination, and fantasy. *Journal of Mental Imagery*, 11:101-113.

Madders, J. (1981). *Stress and Relaxation: Self-Help Ways to Cope With Stress and Relieve Nervous Tension, Ulcers, Insomnia, Migraine, and High Blood Pressure* (3rd ed.). London: Martin Dunitz.

McGuigan, F.J. (1981). *Calm Down: A Guide for Stress and Tension Control*. Englewood Cliffs, NJ: Prentice-Hall

McKay, M., Davis, M., & Eshelman, E.R. (Eds.). (1988). *Relaxation and Stress Workbook* (3rd ed.). Oakland, Calif.: New Haringer.

Meichenaum, D. & Cameron, R. (1983). Stress inoculation training. In Meichenbaum, D. & McCormack G.L. (1992). The therapeutic benefits of the relaxation response. *Occupational Therapy Practice*, 4:51-60.

Mitchell, L. (1987). *Simple Relaxation: The Mitchell Method for Easing Tension* (2nd ed.) London: John Murray.

Morrison, J.B. (1988). Chronic asthma and improvement with relaxation induced by hypnotherapy. *Journal of the Royal Society of Medicine*, 81:701-704.

Neptune, E.C. (1977). An investigation of the effect of meditation training in a cigarette smoking extinguishment programme. *Dissertation Abstracts International*, 39 416B. University microfilms number 7811433.

Ornstein, R.E. (1975). *The Psychology of Consciousness*. Harmondsworth, UK: Penguin.

Ost, L.G. (1987). Applied relaxation: description of a coping technique and review of controlled studies. *Behavior Research and Therapy*, 25:397-407.

Papp, L.A., Klein, D.F., & Gorman, J.M. (1993). Carbon dioxide hypersensitivity, hyperventilation, and panic disorder. *American Journal of Psychiatry*, 150:1149-1157.

Payne, Rosemary A. (1995). *Relaxation Techniques*. Edinburgh: Churchill Livingstone.

Peterson, C. & Bossio, L.M. (1991). *Health and Optimism*. New York: Macmillan.

Peterson, C., Seligman, M.E.P., & Vaillant, G.E. (1988). Pessimistic explanatory style is a risk factor for physical illness: a thirty-five-year longitudinal study. *Journal of Personality and Social Psychology*, 55:23-27.

Rubin, B.K. (1983). *Cognitive, Affective, and Physiological Outcomes of Rebirthing*. Washington D.C.: American University.

Selye, H. (1956). *The Stress of Life*. New York: McGraw-Hill.

Stroebel, C. (1983). Quieting response training. *British Medical Journal*, 287: 387-399.

Zimbardo, P.G., LaBerge, S., and Butler, L.D. (1993). Psychophysiological consequences of unexplained arousal: a posthypnotic suggestion paradigm. *Journal of Abnormal Psychology*. 102(3):466-473.

About the Author

For the past 24 years, **Robert Lawrence Friedman, MA**—author, professional speaker/trainer, and psychotherapist—has provided his keynote presentations, training programs, workshops, and coaching programs to Fortune 100 and 500 corporations, universities, and health-care organizations throughout the United States, Europe, and Asia.

Friedman's expertise in the areas of stress management, leadership development, and teambuilding has led to national and international media attention. He was featured on the year-long Discovery Health Channel documentary, *Class of '75*, in which he mentored five individuals in order to teach them strategies for managing their stress and creating a positive and sustained lifestyle change. Other appearances have included *The Morning Show on Today* (NBC), NY One News, Fox News, E Television, "The Alive and Wellness Show" (CNBC), along with television shows on Fuji and Sankei Television programs in Japan.

Friedman has shared his unique and innovative views in *Alternative Medicine*, *Cosmopolitan*, *Newsday*, *The Washington Times*, and many other publications. He has been the "Stresswise" columnist in *Healthwise* magazine for the past seven years.

Friedman has offered keynote presentations and training programs on stress management and teambuilding to such corporations as Accenture, American Express, BBDO International, Chase Manhattan Bank, CMP Media, Comedy Central, First Boston, Forbes, HBO, Hyatt Hotels, Hoffman-LaRoche, Pitney Bowes, Schering Plough, Saatchi & Saatchi, Shiseido, Standard & Poors, Time-Warner, Viacom, and Xerox, among many others.

Friedman has also provided his workshops to such health-care institutions as Beth Israel Medical Center, Bon Secaur Health Care System, Clara Maass Medical Center, Cornell Medical Center, Irvington General Hospital, Kimball Medical Center, Monmouth Medical Center, Newark Beth Israel Medical Center, New York Hospital, Saint Barnabas Medical Center, Saint Mary's Hospital, Saint Vincent's Hospital, Union Hospital, and West Hudson Hospital for the past five years.

As an approved provider for the National Board for Certified Counselors, Friedman's website (www.stress-solutions.com) provides online interactive courses for individuals seeking to further their education in managing their stress. In addition, he has designed a cutting-edge software program (Relaxation On-Demand, available at www.mypersonaloasis.com) for stressed individuals who are seeking immediate stress relief, and has partnered with his brother, a clinical psychologist and hypnotherapist, to create variations of this "immediate-need" software program using positive psychology for confidence gain and pain management.

Friedman is the author of the breakthrough book *The Healing Power of the Drum: A Psychotherapist Explores the Healing Power of Rhythm*, which investigates the use of rhythm as a teambuilding tool and stress reliever. Healthy Learning has produced 15 of Friedman's workshops and seminars on DVD.

Friedman is a professional member of the National Speaker's Association and the American Counseling Association.

For further information, contact info@stress-solutions.com.

THIS BOOK BELONGS TO:

____

____

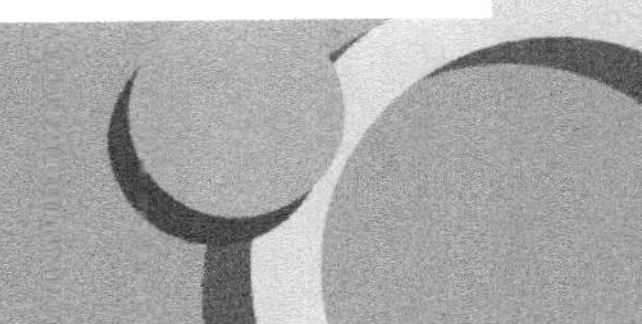

TABLE OF CONTENTS

INTRODUCTION:

This book is designed to help you grow in your relationship with God every week by offering you devotionals that are short, easy to understand, and inspirational. You can read them in order or skip ahead to find a devotional that speaks to your specific situation in any particular week. You can then apply what you learn in each week's devotional to your daily life. This devotional is designed to help teach young boys the importance of having a relationship with God and how knowing Him personally can benefit you. The sooner you start, the faster you will learn about God. Then you can take what you have learned and help teach other people how their lives will change for the best when they give their lives to Christ. Being a preteen or a teenage boy can be some of the most wonderful times of your life. So many different things demand your attention every day which can test your commitment/availability to have a personal relationship with God. Things that demand your attention can include but aren't limited to making and keeping friends, working out or playing a sport, feeling the pressure of performing during sports, facing puberty, changing schools, struggling with tests and projects in school, mentoring your brothers and sisters, helping your parents clean the house, and making sure that you spend time winding down after school every day.

HOW TO USE THIS BOOK:

You can use this book to strengthen your relationship with God by reading a devotional every week. Each week is filled with inspiring and uplifting stories that help young boys learn more about who they are in Christ, their place in this world, and how they can be a positive impact in the world. There are short, easy-to-understand five-minute devotional lessons that you can get into the habit of reading every week. Sometimes, you might have to read a devotional more than once for it to really sink in. That's what we suggest! After you read each devotional, you can have personal prayer time to connect with God and talk to Him about what you have read. Some of the topics include: Honoring God with your talents, obeying your parents, navigating challenging times at school, teamwork, making smart choices, as well as other lessons that you will learn as a young boy. There are prayers that pertain to each week's lesson that will help you grow your relationship with God. This book will help you navigate all the different phases of your life as you grow into the man of God that He created you to be. It is our hope that this book gives boys the joy, strength, and confidence they need to enjoy their lives to the fullest as they follow after Jesus and discover the call he has for them.

PRESSURE BEING A PRETEEN BOY

"Blessed is the one who perseveres under trial because, having stood the test, that person will receive the crown of life that the Lord has promised to those who love him." James 1:12 NIV

Ten-year-old Michael walked into the kitchen and slammed his school bag on the chair. Grandpa looked up from his paper. "What's wrong buddy?" He asked. Michael flopped on the couch next to him and explained. "I'm really struggling with math and I have a test on Friday. I need to understand it before then but I know the test will be tough." Grandpa put his big arm around Michael and said, "Math is difficult for a lot of boys your age. You're not alone. But God will help you do your best. No matter what, believe in yourself. You will be very proud of yourself for persevering even though math is tough and stresses you out. When you persevere through the test, it doesn't matter what grade you get, God is proud of you for your effort and endurance." Michael was encouraged by this and asked, "Grandpa, can we pray together that God helps me do my best?" Grandpa took Michael's hand and said a prayer with him. A week later, Michael came home smiling. "Grandpa look! I tried my best and persevered! I got a B on the test!" God promises you that you will receive the crown of life because you know God. The next time you persevere through something tough, like any school tests, you will be proud of yourself, but God is even more proud of your character and effort to persevere. He will help you to try your best every day no matter what you face.

WEEKLY PRAYER

Dear God, please help me to persevere through any tests and trials that come my way. Some will be small and others will be large but I trust you to help me through all of them. Thank you for your kindness in guiding me when sometimes I feel lost. Amen.

MY PRAYER

WEEK 2

HONORING GOD WITH YOUR TALENTS

"Whatever you do, work at it with all your heart, as working for the Lord, not for human masters." Colossians 3:23 NIV

Nine-year-old David came running into the backyard where his mom was watering her plants. "Mom! Guess what. I get to help light the candles during chapel at school next week. I'm really excited but I'm a bit nervous." "That's great David. How great you get to volunteer lighting candles at church," said Mom. "We can practice with you lighting the candles on our mantle tonight and throughout the week," she said. "You don't have to be nervous. All you have to do is remember that you are doing everything for the glory of God, not for other people." Over the next week, David and his mom practiced lighting the candles on the mantle and each night he was getting better and gaining more confidence. The morning of chapel, David hugged his mom and she said, "Just do your best, you have practiced and are prepared to light the candles." David took a deep breath and as chapel started he walked up to the front of the room to light the candles. He knew he was honoring God and that God was with Him. He was able to light all of the candles on the first try. No mistakes. No matter what you do in school, at home, or in church, you're honoring God whenever you work at something with all of your heart. Whenever you work at something, work as if you're serving the Lord, it won't feel like work. Rather, it'll feel like an honor to do anything and everything for the Lord.

WEEKLY PRAYER

Dear God, please help me to honor you with all of my talents and any opportunities I get to use them. Help me to work at everything I do with all of my heart and keep my eyes on serving you, not others. I want you to be the focus of everything I do. Amen

MY PRAYER

WEEK 3

MAKING SMART CHOICES

" Trust in the Lord with all your heart. And lean not on your own understanding; in all your ways submit to him, and he will make your paths straight." Proverbs 3:5-6 NIV

Twelve-year-old Andy was having trouble keeping friends. The kids he usually sat with at lunch started to make fun of him and didn't want to sit with him anymore. He didn't understand why they didn't like him anymore and he just wanted his friends back. He tried saying something nice to them, sharing his lunch, and even invited the kids to sit with him. However, they still continued to make fun of him and call him names. His teacher Ms. Rose took notice and asked Andy what was going on. "Those kids used to like me. Now they're mean to me, I don't understand what I did wrong," said Andy. Ms. Rose told him that even though he wanted to still be friends with them, it was a good idea to talk to God about it. "Remember the verse we learned? Trust in the Lord with all of your heart and lean not on your own understanding...He will make your paths straight. God can help you make smarter choices about who you are friends with," said Ms. Rose. Andy started praying that he would find true friends and trusted in God that he would answer his prayer. Two weeks later, Ms. Rose saw Andy sitting with some new friends and they were having heaps of fun, telling stories and laughing at the lunch table. Andy praised God for giving him true friends. Just like Andy, you can pray that God gives you true friends in your life too.

WEEKLY PRAYER

Dear God, please help me to lean on you and not my own understanding. I want to trust in you, especially when it feels like I am alone. Thank you for making my paths straight and any time I am feeling lonely, let me find comfort in you and friendship with those that are good for me. Thank you for the future you have created for me where I know I will find lots of joy, purpose, and peace. Amen.

MY PRAYER

RESPECTING YOUR PARENTS

"Children, obey your parents in everything, for this pleases the Lord." Colossians 3:20 NIV

Nine-year-old Ronnie was playing video games in the living room when his mom called him to set the table for dinner. Instead of going to the kitchen to set the table, he ignored his mom. A second time his mom called him to set the table. Ronnie still didn't do as he was asked. His dad walked into the living room and asked Ronnie to do what his mom asked him. "Why? I'm playing my game," said Ronnie. His dad knelt down next to him and asked, "Do you remember the Bible verse you and I read last night? It said obey your parents in everything for this pleases the Lord. That includes setting the table when mom asks you to." Ronnie turned his game off and said to his dad, "That seems like such a little thing. I thought the purpose of the scripture was to obey your parents in the bigger things in life." His dad smiled and replied, "When you obey mom and I when we ask you to do the little things, like setting the table, it will help you to want to obey us when we ask you to do bigger things in life." Ronnie nodded and went to set the table. As they sat down to eat dinner, Ronnie apologized to his mom for not obeying her earlier in the night. You know it pleases God when you obey your parents. Next time you are asked to set the table, clean your room, look after your younger brother or sister or even go to bed, know that God is smiling because you obeyed your parents.

WEEKLY PRAYER

Dear God, please help me to obey my parents the first time they ask me to do something. I want to please you in everything I do and it can begin by honoring and obeying them. Thank you for the family I am in and that you see me as your son too. Amen.

MY PRAYER

RESPECTING AUTHORITY

"Have confidence in your leaders and submit to their authority, because they keep watch over you..." Hebrews 13:17 NIV

Mom, how do I know God hears me?" Jennifer asked. "Lately it's as if He doesn't want to listen to me. Am I doing something wrong?" She inquired. "No sweetie. You're not doing anything wrong," mom said. She sat next to Jennifer and pulled out her Bible. "One of my favorite verses is Mathew 7:7. It says, "Ask and it will be given to you, seek and you will find, knock and the door will be opened to you." God wants you to believe that the things you pray for will be given to you. When you seek God, you will find Him. When you knock, the doors of heaven will be opened to you. You may not get the answers you expect, but He knows exactly what you need when you need it," said mom. "So, I can really ask Him for a brother or sister?" Jennifer said. "You can ask Him for anything. As long as it's His will, He will give it to you," said mom. Later that night, Jennifer asked God to give her a sibling if it was His will. Later that month, her mom told her that she was going to be having a baby. Jennifer was ecstatic that she was going to have a sibling. You too can remember that when you seek Him, you will find Him in the most surprising ways. When you knock on the doors of heaven, they will be opened in different ways. Whatever you ask God for, He is willing, ready and able to hear you and will answer you in His timing and in His ways.

WEEKLY PRAYER

Dear God, please help me to know you and to know and respect those people who are in authority over my life. Thank you for my parents, teachers, coaches, family members, and my pastor. Thank you that I get to know you through their Godly guidance and leadership. Amen.

MY PRAYER

NAVIGATING FRIENDSHIP CHANGES

"A friend loves at all times, and a brother is born for a time of adversity."
Proverbs 17:17 NIV

Elijah's friends made fun of him for having a relationship with God. He prayed that God would lead him to good people that would become his friends. His grandma told him that God would answer his prayer and give him the friends that he needed. Later that week, a boy named Daniel approached Elijah and told him that he respected him for his faith in God. As they sat together at lunch, kids made fun of Elijah for praying before he ate his meal. Daniel stood up for Elijah. "He loves God and so do I. Our faith is what makes us strong. Stop making fun of Elijah, he's my friend. Daniel was brave, and bold and defended Elijah. Elijah smiled, thanking both God and Daniel for being there for him. When he got to his grandparent's house, he told his grandma about how Daniel stood up for him. "That's amazing, my grandson. God sent Daniel to stand up for you," said grandma. "The Bible says that a friend loves at all times and a brother is born for a time of adversity. I prayed for you to find a true friend that would stand up for you. God answered my prayer through Daniel." Daniel became like a brother to Elijah. They continued to share their faith with each other and other people. "Thank you for being a true friend, Daniel. Thank you for being there during my time of adversity," said Elijah. God will also give you the right friends in His timing and in His ways. Trust Him to bring them to you when you need them most.

WEEKLY PRAYER

Dear God, please help me to find true friends that will love me, encourage me, and defend me. I want to be brave and bold and share my faith when others question it or see me as different. Help me to speak your truth over my life and the lives of others. I thank you for friends that will make me a better young man. Amen.

MY PRAYER

CHANGING SCHOOLS

'I the Lord do not change. . . "Malachi 3:6 NIV

Eleven-year-old Mason shed tears as he heard the news that he and his family would have to move to a new state. His dad had taken a new job that he couldn't say 'no' to. Mason was sad that he would have to leave his school where he made so many good Christian, Godly friends. In his new school he struggled to make friends. He wished that he would have his Christian friends back, but found it hard trusting God.

One day while he was visiting his family, he asked his Aunt Becky why it was so hard for him when he changed schools. "Changing schools can be difficult for anybody, especially you as a young boy. Even though you miss your old friends, there is a true friend that will never change. Do you know who it is?" asked Aunt Becky. "Yeah I do, it's Jesus?" replied Mason. "Yes. God will never change. He loves you. You are a child of the most high God, Mason!" said Aunt Becky. Even though it's hard to change schools, you too can cling to God because He never changes.

WEEKLY PRAYER

Dear God please help me to remember that despite the ever-changing circumstances of my life, you never change. Thank you for being the same yesterday, today and forever. I want to be thankful towards you because you never vary even though I do. Thank you for your kindness towards me each and every day. Amen.

MY PRAYER

CHALLENGES IN HIGH SCHOOL

"For I am the Lord your God. Who takes hold of your right hand. And says to you, Do not fear; I will help you."
Isaiah 41:13 NIV

Peter was nervous about starting high school. He didn't know what to expect. He told his Uncle Mark how he felt. "High school was tough for me too. It's tough for everybody in many different ways. But God doesn't want you to live with anxiety and fear over what you will face in high school," said Uncle Mark. Uncle Mark continued explaining that God wanted Peter to know that He loves him and watches over him. "He takes hold of you with His righteous right hand," said Uncle Mark. He is the Lord your God. He even says to not fear anything because He is always willing to help you." When you feel afraid you can turn to God in prayer and talk to Him about whatever challenges you face in high school. You can ask Him to help you not be afraid of any of the changes in your life. Even though you will face difficulties in high school, there is nothing that you can't beat when God is with you and at your side. Whether you struggle with your grades, fitness in sports, or you are finding it tough to make friends, you can turn to God in prayer and ask Him for His help at any time, for any reason. There's nothing He won't help you overcome. You will be able to overcome any and every obstacle in high school.

WEEKLY PRAYER

Dear God, please help me to be brave, bold, and faith-filled. I do not want to fear any challenges that I face in school. Thank you for always being there for me and wanting to see me faith-filled and not fear-driven.
Amen.

MY PRAYER

SPORTS TEAM STRUGGLES

"Similarly, anyone who competes as an athlete does not receive the victor's crown except by competing according to the rules." 2 Timothy 2:5 NIV

Frankie raced around the bases at his baseball game. He loved playing baseball and getting to know his teammates and coaches. As he came sliding into home plate, he didn't hear the empire yell "SAFE!" Instead, he heard the empire yell "OUT!" Frankie was angry after he had been practicing so hard to help his team win games. "Oh, come on! You know that I was safe! I slid into home before I got tagged!" shouted Frankie. "This isn't fair. I was the fastest one out there!" "Sorry Frankie. You're out," said his coach. "Everyone on the team is helping us play better together. You're not the only one trying to help us win. You have to play by the rules and remember that this is a team sport. Anyone who competes as an athlete won't receive the victory unless you compete by the rules." "Ok coach, I got it. Can I talk to the team?" asked Frankie. The coach nodded. Frankie took a deep breath, calmed himself and said "Come on guys, we can win this game if we work together! I apologize for disagreeing with the referee. Everybody be your best, play your part in the team and we will all do our best to win." The coach loved seeing Frankie lead the team with this new attitude.

Think about your favorite team sport that you love to play. At times you will struggle with staying humble. There might even be times when you think your abilities are keeping the team from losing, but it's more about the team working together. Team sports and competitions will help you learn the importance of teamwork. God will help you work together with your teammates. Being humble is more important than boasting about your athletic abilities.

WEEKLY PRAYER

Dear God, please help me to not be prideful or boastful about my abilities as an athlete. Help me to be humble about the talents you have given me. Let me use them to glorify you. I want to be honest when I compete because I am representing you in everything I do. Amen.

MY PRAYER

WEEK 10

LOOKING FOR MALE MENTORS

"As iron sharpens iron. So, one person sharpens another."
Proverbs 27:17 NIV

William just wanted to be close to his dad. He looked up to him and admired him. But his dad always seemed to be too busy to spend time with him. He wished that his dad would want to spend time with him. He decided to ask his teacher, Mr Pearson for advice because he knew he could trust him. "Excuse me sir, can I ask your advice about something?" William asked. "Sure buddy. What's up?" answered Mr Pearson. "I really want to be close to my dad but he doesn't want to be close to me. I really want him to coach me and teach me things," said William. "What can I do?" "Well buddy, sometimes dads are so busy with their work and taking care of things at the house that they forget the importance of spending quality time with their kids. But there are a lot of other people that can be your male mentors like your coaches, uncles, teachers," said Mr Pearson. William smiled at him and asked, "Can you be my mentor, someone I look up to and can help me make good choices for my life?" Mr Pearson was humbled, but impressed by William's maturity and honesty. "Sure kiddo, but I'm not going to take your dad's place. One day, your dad will see how important it is for him to spend time with you," said Mr Pearson. He prayed that William's dad would want to spend time with him. You can pray that your dad wants to spend more time with you too.

WEEKLY PRAYER

Dear God, please help me to know who I can and can't turn to as my male mentors in my life. I know I am going to need Godly advice and wisdom from men that can encourage me. Please provide the right mentor or coach for me to learn from as I get older. Amen.

MY PRAYER

ABSENT FATHERS

"A father to the fatherless, a defender of widows, is God in his holy dwelling." Psalm 68:7 NIV

Bobby longed to have a family like everyone else did. He saw his friends having great relationships with their dads and wished that he could have that same relationship with his dad. He remembered the verse he read in Sunday school that Jesus is the father to the fatherless. He got on his knees and prayed that God would work in his relationship with his dad. Later in the week his dad was working on his car in the garage and Bobby walked up to him. "Hey dad. Can I help you with your car?" He asked. His dad turned around and smiled. "Sure, you can help me," he said. As they started working on the car together his dad apologized for not spending enough time with Bobby. "It's ok dad. I knew God would help us get closer to each other again," said Bobby. He silently thanked God for allowing his dad and him to start talking together again. You too can come to your heavenly father for anything in your life and talk to Him. Even if you're struggling with a relationship with your dad, ask God to help you know what to say and do to start renewing that relationship. It might take more time than you expect, but God will hopefully restore the relationship if it's in His will. He is the father to the fatherless and a defender of the widows. He can help bring peace in your heart towards your father if you feel like he has been absent at times.

WEEKLY PRAYER

Dear God, please help me to always seek you as my heavenly father every day. Thank you that you are always here for me and that you defend me. Thank you for putting peace in my heart and I ask for grace over my relationships, especially the one I have with my earthly father. Amen.

MY PRAYER

REBELLING AS A TEEN

"A rod and a reprimand impart wisdom. But a child left undisciplined disgraces its mother." Proverbs 29:15 NIV

Jakob slammed the door right in his mother's face. She had just asked him to clean his room before coming down for dinner. Jakob yelled at his mother "You are always asking me to clean up and I hate doing it. I hate it so much!" Jakob's mother told him he was grounded for a week for being rude and disrespectful. Jakob texted his friend that he was grounded. His friend texted back, "Come on dude. Just sneak out and come to my house. Who cares what your mom says!" Jakob climbed out his bedroom window and jumped to the ground. When he got to his friend's house, they started playing video games. When Jakob's mom called him for dinner, he didn't come downstairs. She walked into his room and realized that he'd snuck out. She called his mobile. "You get home right now young man! You not only disrespected me but disobeyed me!" Even though he didn't want to, Jakob went home. He started cleaning his room immediately. His mom walked in and said, "Jakob, thank you for cleaning your room. I don't discipline you to make you hate me. I do it to teach you what God wants you to know. The Bible says a child without discipline disgraces his mother." Those words stung Jakob's heart. He didn't want to disgrace or disrespect his mother. He asked for her forgiveness. Whenever you feel like disobeying your mom, remember that it's better to honor what she asks you to do. You're not only honoring her, but you are also honoring God.

WEEKLY PRAYER

Dear God, please help me to obey my parents and honor them, so I can honor you. I do not want to disgrace my mother in any way, so please help me to be more respectful and appreciative of all she does for me. I am blessed to honor you by honoring others. Please let me learn from my mistakes and see the wisdom when I have been reprimanded or disciplined. Amen.

MY PRAYER

WEEK 13

DATING

"*Do not be yoked together with unbelievers.*" 2 Corinthians 6:14 NIV

Mark just wanted a girlfriend. He tried to impress the girls at his school. One girl he dated didn't know Jesus as her Savior and every time he spent time with her, Mark felt the Holy Spirit was communicating with him that he was only supposed to be friends with her. Nothing more than that. He then asked his good friend, Pastor John about the Holy Spirit's voice. "Well Mark it says in the Bible to not be yoked with an unbeliever. Those promptings of the Holy Spirit are not random. God is telling you to move on from that girl because of your differences in faith, morals and beliefs" said Pastor John. "Wow! That's deep. Can we pray together that He leads me to find the right girl in my life at the right time?" Pastor John smiled, put his hands on Mark's shoulder and began to pray. Mark broke up with his girlfriend and instead focused on spending more time with God and listening to the Holy Spirit's voice. Mark noticed that as the year went on he was interested in becoming friends with girls that had the same faith, beliefs and morals as him. You too can pray that God will help highlight girls he wants you to be friends with and who believe in the same things as you. He hears any and all of your prayers, even ones about getting a girlfriend.

WEEKLY PRAYER

Dear God, please help me to find a girl that loves you, when the time is right. Help me to continue to grow in my relationship with you and give me the character and integrity to make you proud. I want to honor you in my relationships with girls and that one day when I am ready you will bless me with the one perfect for me. Amen.

MY PRAYER

WEEK 14

HELPING OTHERS

"...not looking to your own interests but each of you to the interests of the others." Philippians 2:4 NIV

Johnny came home and saw his little sister Jessie sleeping on the couch. He turned on the TV and started playing his video game. A minute later Jessie woke up asking him to turn off the TV. "No way. I need to relax," he complained. "I came home from school today because I'm sick. Can you please turn off the TV?" Jessie kindly asked. Johnny shook his head. "Do you ever think of anyone but yourself?" Jessie protested. "Didn't you learn anything in our Sunday school lesson about thinking of others above yourself?" Johnny glared at her as Jessie got off the couch and went to her room. His dad walked into the living room. "Johnny, your sister hasn't been feeling good. You should have waited to play your video game. Why don't you try and make it better?" said dad. "Oh, come on dad!" Johnny whinged. "Nope! Go apologize to your sister," said dad. Johnny shut off his game and went into his sister's room. "Hey sis," he said. "What can I do to help you feel better?" "Can you bring me the heating pad?" Jessie asked. Johnny nodded. As he went to get the heating pad, he started to realize how good it felt to put her needs before his. "I'm sorry I didn't listen when you told me you needed the couch," he said. Jessie thanked him for thinking of her. You too can look for ways to be there for your siblings instead of thinking about yourself.

WEEKLY PRAYER

Dear God, help me to seek out opportunities to help others, instead of only wanting to help myself. You have given me siblings and friends to show them your love, give me the heart to put their needs before my own. That's what you would do . . . and I want to be more like you. Amen.

MY PRAYER

SIBLING RIVALRY

"Whoever claims to love God yet hates a brother or sister is a liar. For whoever does not love their brother and sister, whom they have seen, cannot love God, whom they have not seen." 1 John 4:20 NIV

As Hunter was studying for his test, his sister Georgie came running into his room and started bouncing on his bed. "Do you mind? I'm trying to study," Hunter yelled. Georgie continued to run around his room and knocked over his favorite Lego car creation. "What did you do?! You broke my Lego collection! I spent all week working on this! Get out of my room! I hate you!" Hunter yelled. His sister ran out of the room crying. "Why did you just tell your sister you hate her?" Asked his mom. "It's never ok to tell anyone that you hate them, especially your siblings." "Oh, come on mom! I didn't really mean it. She's just so annoying, that's all," said Hunter. "Then you need to apologize to her, take it back and tell her that you definitely don't hate her," said his mom. "Do you remember the verse we read over the weekend? Anyone who claims they love God but says they hate their sibling is a liar." Hunter nodded and went to his sister's room to make up with her. "I take it back Georgie, I don't hate you. I just really needed to study for this test and those words came out. I definitely didn't mean it," he said. "Well can I help you study for the test by quizzing you? I want to help you get a good grade," said Georgie. "OK! Awesome! Thanks for being willing to help me sis!" Hunter thanked God for his sister's forgiveness and that she was willing to help him study. Think back to a time when you said harmful and careless words to your sibling. You know you can repair that relationship with God's help and find ways to enjoy spending time with your siblings.

WEEKLY PRAYER

Dear God, please help me to love my siblings instead of fighting with them. I don't want to say things that are harmful or careless. I want them to know I love them because I love you. Show me how to love them better and give me patience when they are annoying. Amen.

MY PRAYER

WEEK 16

DO EVEYRTHING FOR CHRIST

"So whether you eat or drink or whatever you do, do it all for the glory of God." 1 Corinthians 10:31 NIV

Leo was reading his Bible at the kitchen table. "How's the devotional time going buddy?" asked dad. "It's interesting, but I don't understand something," said Leo. His dad pulled up a chair as Leo began to explain, "This Bible verse talks about doing everything for the glory of God. But does it really mean everything? How am I supposed to do everything for the glory of God?" It was a great question. Leo's dad answered, "Well, when you get a drink of water you can thank God for giving you the gift of water. Whenever you eat your favorite food or a snack, you can also give thanks for being able to eat at least three meals per day. Not everyone has those blessings and provisions. But this verse doesn't just mean thanking Him for the provision of every meal you have and every drink that you drink. It also means honoring God in the way you speak, think and act every day. He knows that you're not perfect, so you don't have to try to be perfect. He wants you to make the effort to think about how you can live life for Him. That means whether you're eating or drinking something, or when you see a friend who needs a hand with their schoolwork, you can offer to help them," said his dad. You too can do everything in your daily life for Christ, whether you eat, drink, speak to a friend, clean your room, or just give your sibling a hug.

WEEKLY PRAYER

Dear God, please help me to do everything for you. I want to remember every day that you have created me uniquely but ultimately I have been purpose-designed to reflect you in all that I do. Thank you that I have the privilege of living my life for you every day. Amen

MY PRAYER

MAKING CHURCH A PRIORITY

"I rejoiced with those who said to me, "Let us go to the house of the Lord." Psalm 122:1 NIV

Kurt was eating his cereal in front of the TV. "Why aren't you dressed for church?" asked his mom. "Why do we have to go every weekend? Can't we just stay here and watch TV and hang out as a family?" complained Kurt. Mom explained that going to church every week was one of the main priorities of their family. "Even though you may not always want to go to church with us, you have to start thinking about church and how important it is to go," said mom. Kurt shut off the TV and got dressed for church. At church, Pastor Tom explained how a relationship with God is the most valuable part of our lives. The pastor explained that life is made up of high times and low times, anything could happen at any time. It's so important to keep God first in your life. "Even though it can be tough to go to church every week, we can find freedom within the community of believers that worship together and seek after God together," said Pastor Tom. After the service, Kurt was filled with curiosity and conviction and asked Pastor Tom to pray with him about making church a priority in his life. He prayed that God would help him to be open in his heart to learn more about Him every day. After that Sunday Kurt worked hard to spend more time with God each day. It got easier and easier for him to go to church each week too. Going to church becomes fun when you make it about being part of a faith-filled com-

WEEKLY PRAYER

Dear God, please help me to pray in any and every circumstance. Thank you that I can talk to You any time I want to. I want to be constantly praying and talking to you no matter how busy I get.
Amen.

MY PRAYER

WHAT'S YOUR PASSION? NATURE

"Flee the evil desires of youth and pursue righteousness, faith, love and peace, along with those who call on the Lord out of a pure heart." 2 Timothy 2:22 NIV

Taylor was at the basketball court making some shots when his friend Nick came to join him. The two boys played basketball against each other and after some time sat on the bench and started talking about God. Nick said that he had a passion for playing basketball but didn't know how God would use that passion to change the world through him. Taylor saw this as an opportunity to tell Nick that God is capable of anything. "If you want to, Nick, we can always talk later about this because this is a huge conversation that may take time," he said. "Thanks Taylor," said Nick. Later that evening Nick came over to Taylor's parent's house. "Taylor, I love basketball so much, but I also want to serve God with my whole life," Nick said. "How do I do that?" Taylor was encouraged by Nick's question and helped him understand further by sharing this, "Following passions without God can make life harder, but asking God to be in the middle of your passions can help you make a difference in the world. "You can still pursue basketball, but make sure to put God first in your life," said Taylor. "Remember how our teacher told us to let go of our youthful desires and pursue faith, love, peace and even righteousness?" "Yeah. I remember. Can we pray together?" asked Nick. "Sure," said Taylor and prayed this great prayer, "Dear Lord, you know we both love basketball, but please help us to include you every day in everything we do. In Jesus' name we pray and we believe it. Amen."

WEEKLY PRAYER

Dear God, please help me to pursue the passions that you have put in my heart. You have given them to me because you know I find joy and happiness in them. I want to find how I can use my passions to glorify you. Help me in this and let me see clearly the unique design you have for my life. Amen.

MY PRAYER

BEING A ROLE MODEL

"In everything set them an example by doing what is good. In your teaching show integrity, seriousness."
Titus 2:7 NIV

"Go Brandon! You got this bro!" yelled his older brother Ricky as Brandon was playing in his first football game. He really enjoyed cheering Brandon on from the sidelines. His dad noticed how attentive Ricky was at Brandon's games. "I really admire your attitude at Brandon's games, Ricky," said dad. "It means a lot to see you supporting him as he tries a new sport." "You guys always taught me to set an example for him," said Ricky. As Brandon ran to the sidelines after the game, Ricky gave him a high five and squeezed him in his arms. "I saw the tackle you made buddy. Great job," said Ricky. "Thanks bro. I'm still struggling with passing the ball. Can you help me?" asked Brandon. Ricky nodded. The next day he saw Brandon relaxing in front of the TV. "Come on. Let's go outside and practice," Ricky said. "Oh come on Ricky, can't we play video games today?" asked Brandon. Ricky took a deep breath. "You asked me to help you get better at passing. The only way to get better is to practice," said Ricky. Brandon agreed with Ricky. He started by throwing the ball very close to Brandon and then moved further away. The practice paid off. Every day Brandon got better at throwing the football and at the next game he threw a pass to a teammate and helped score a touchdown. You can be a great example too for any of your younger siblings or friends. Just find something that they need help with and be kind enough to take the time to show them and teach them.

WEEKLY PRAYER

Dear God, thank you for creating me to be an example. I want to help others be their best, so please use me to be a role model to my younger siblings and anyone else that needs help. I want to share your love with them, so that they may feel it when you use me to be an example. Amen.

MY PRAYER

WEEK 20

LOOK UP TO YOUR FATHER

"Follow my example, as I follow the example of Christ."
1 Corinthians 11:1 NIV

Sam saw his dad washing the dishes after dinner because his mom wasn't feeling good. After his dad did the dishes, he started to fold the laundry. He saw how much his dad was doing around the house and felt like he wanted to help him out. Sam asked if he could make some tea for his mom to help her feel better. "Sure buddy. You can make the tea and after I'm done folding the clothes I'm going to give her the medicine. "I can take it to her when I bring her the tea," Sam offered. "I know your mom will appreciate it," said dad. As his dad continued to fold the clothes Sam made his mom tea and brought her the medicine. "I'm so sorry I haven't been able to do too much the past few days," said his mom. Sam told her not to worry. "Dad and I have it all taken care of, mom. You just rest up and let us know if you need anything else, ok?" said Sam. Smiling, his mom thanked him. Later that night she told his dad how happy it made her that he was showing Sam how to help out around the house. "I want to live by Jesus' example so that way Sam sees Christ through my actions," said dad. As he said goodnight to Sam, he thanked him for helping him and for taking good care of his mom. You can follow your earthly father's example too when you see him acting as Christ would take care of others.

WEEKLY PRAYER

Dear God, please give me good Christ-like examples to look up to. I already seek to know you more as my Heavenly Father, but if there are things my dad does that I can learn from, please make it nice and clear for me to see. Speak to my heart in those moments. Thank you for the example that Jesus gives us to love others. Amen.

MY PRAYER

LOOK TO YOUR HEAVENLY FATHER

"But just as he who called you is holy, so be holy in all you do;"
1 Peter 1:15 NIV

"It is important to be Jesus' example in everything you say and do," said Mr. Roberts as he was teaching his religion class. A boy named Frank raised his hand. "Mr. Roberts, how can we be holy when we sin every day? Jesus is the only one who was holy," Frank said. "Well Frank, even though you sin every day, you can be and are forgiven by God. He called you to be a witness to everyone in your life and to help them know Him," said Mr. Roberts. He continued to explain to the class that each student is holy and precious in God's eyes. "When you asked Jesus to come into your heart, you were saved. He sacrificed His life when He died on the cross for your sins. You are made holy when you have a relationship with God," said Mr. Roberts. He encouraged his class to look to Jesus as the perfect example. "So all I have to do to be holy is keep my relationship with God first in my life?" asked Frank. Mr. Roberts nodded yes. Frank said he couldn't wait to tell other people in his life about God. You too can be holy and lead others to Christ.

WEEKLY PRAYER

Dear God, thank you for loving me and saving me with your salvation. Please help me to look up to you and to be your example in everything I say and do. Help me to be holy in my words and actions, even when others are not. Let your Holy Spirit guide me in those moments. Amen.

MY PRAYER

DEALING WITH ANXIETY

"Cast all your anxiety on him because he cares for you."
1 Peter 5:7 NIV

Howard was pacing the kitchen wondering if he made the soccer team after all of the practice he put in. His older sister Jennifer came into the kitchen and put her arm around him. " You did your best, bro. That's all you can do. I know you really want to make the varsity team. No matter what happens, mom, dad and I are proud of you,' said Jennifer. "Thanks sis. I'm so nervous to find out if I made it or not. We don't find out until Wednesday," said Howard. Jennifer explained to him that he didn't have to live with anxiety in his heart. Instead he could give it all to God. "You can cast all of your anxiety on God at any time, whether it's day or night because He loves you and cares for you," Jennifer reminded him. Howard bowed his head and prayed that God would calm his emotions and worry about making the varsity soccer team. Whenever you face anxiety in your life whether it's about trying out for a sports team or student leadership teams, or about a big project in school, you can give all your worries to God. He doesn't want you to carry the burden of anxiety every day. Instead, He wants you to put your anxiety on His shoulders because He cares for you.

WEEKLY PRAYER

Dear God, please help me find peace by giving you my worry and anxiety if I'm ever faced with it. I trust you to cast all of my anxiety on you. Thank you for caring about me enough to take the weight of certain pressures of of my shoulders every day. I love you and find comfort in you. Amen.

MY PRAYER

WEEK 23

DON'T START FIGHTS

"A hot-tempered person stirs up conflict, but the one who is patient calms a quarrel." Proverbs 15:18 NIV

Justin was tired of being bullied at school. A few boys in his class called him a nerd because he was always reading. He sighed as he got into his grandma's car when she picked him up from school. "Hey Justin. How was school?" Grandma Pip asked. "Not good. There are kids bullying me and I really want to get even with them," said Justin. "What are they making fun of you for?" asked Grandma Pip. Justin explained that some boys were making fun of him because he was always reading. "Just because I love reading and learning new things doesn't make me a nerd. I really want to make fun of them for being dumb." Grandma Pip explained to him that that was not the answer and it was better for Justin to ignore them. "Really? Why not?" asked Justin. In a calming voice and soft tone, Grandma Pip answered, "In the Bible, it says a person who is hot-tempered stirs up conflict but one who is patient calms a quarrel." She explained that it would be better for him to be nice to the kids who were bullying him or just ignore them. "You really think that will work? Ok, I'll try it," said Justin. The next day at school, a couple of boys started to say mean things to Justin, but instead of fighting with them Justin smiled at them and told them to have a nice day. Justin felt great that their words did not impact him or stick to him.

If kids are bullying you, you can calmly respond to them, or ignore them and avoid starting a fight. You will need to have lots of patience, but definitely tell an adult you trust what is happening and let them help you. Don't ever accept being bullied, tell someone you trust and ask them for help if it is hurting you.

WEEKLY PRAYER

Dear God, I want to love others, but it is hard when I am being bullied. Give me strength, patience and resilience to defend myself and tell an adult if needs be. I want to be calm even if someone hurts me with their words or actions. But I also know it hurts your heart when we are not kind to each other. Give me the grace to be kind to others when they are not kind to me. Amen.

MY PRAYER

WEEK 24

DO NOT WORRY

"When anxiety was great within me, your consolation brought me joy." Psalm 94:19 NIV

As Jeremy ran to score a goal, he felt a sharp pain in his right knee. He was able to score the goal for his team but then collapsed in pain. His coach and parents ran toward him. "My knee! It hurts so bad!" he cried out. His coach knelt beside him. When he touched Jeremy's knee he screamed in pain. "You'll be ok son," said Jeremy's dad. He then dialed 9-1-1 because Jeremy couldn't even sit or stand up. As the ambulance arrived by the soccer field Jeremy was worried and asked if he could ever play soccer again. After examining him at the hospital, the doctor came into his hospital room and told Jeremy and his parents the news. "You tore a ligament in your knee. You won't be able to play soccer for the remainder of the season. I'm sorry," the doctor said. Jeremy broke down crying, but his mom whispered encouragement. "You will be a better soccer player after this than you were before," she said. Later that night she read him a Bible verse while laying hands on his injury. The Bible verse was "When anxiety was great within me, your consolation brought me joy." Psalm 94: 19. He thanked his mom for her encouragement. With therapy, Jeremy was able to get back on the soccer field before the end of the season, sooner than expected and his team was thrilled to have him back. Whenever you feel discouraged or let down, remember that God will bring you the joy and encouragement you need to get through it.

WEEKLY PRAYER

Dear God, please help me not to worry about anything. Help me to turn to you the next time I feel anxiety rising up within me. Please turn my anxiety into joy and then let me give thanks to you for how you have given me freedom because my hope is in you. I want to always fix my eyes on you and not on my pain. Amen.

MY PRAYER

ENCOURAGE OTHERS

"Therefore encourage one another and build each other up, just as in fact you are doing." 1 Thessalonians 5:11 NIV

Cooper saw his sister struggling to ride her bike without training wheels. Instead of helping her feel better, he just started laughing at her. "You're eight years old and you can't ride a bike without training wheels?" he teased. "Hey! It's harder than it looks!" yelled his sister Dani. Their Uncle Frank came out into the front yard and told Cooper that it wasn't nice to make fun of his sister. Cooper rolled his eyes at Uncle Frank. "How would you like it if your sister made fun of you for struggling to ride a bike?" asked Uncle Frank. "But I already know how to ride my bike. So, I don't have to worry about that," said Cooper. "Ok well how'd you like it if I made fun of you for struggling to pass science?" asked Dani. "What's your point?" said Cooper. Uncle Frank explained that it was much better for them to encourage each other than to tear each other down. Cooper turned to Dani and asked what he could do to help her. "I need help balancing. Can you hold me while I pedal my bike?" asked Dani. Cooper nodded and Dani started pedaling down the driveway while Cooper held onto her bike. After multiple attempts, she told him to let go and she was able to ride her bike up and down the street without his help and without training wheels. "Yay sis! You did it!" Cooper yelled. You can encourage your siblings and build them up just like Cooper did.

WEEKLY PRAYER

Dear God, please help me to encourage my family and friends in the same way you have encouraged me. Thank you for giving me the opportunity to build people up every day. Help me to see opportunities for this and give me the kindness to speak life into those around me. Amen.

MY PRAYER

WEEK 26

DON'T SPEAK NEGATIVELY ABOUT YOURSELF

"Gracious words are a honeycomb, sweet to the soul and healing to the bones." Proverbs 16:24 NIV

Reggie was stunned when he found out that he would have to move because his mom had gotten a new job. He had just become best friends with a kid named Tyson and didn't want to leave. "Why do you have to leave?" asked Tyson. "I'm going to miss you so much! I can't believe I won't get to see you every day." "I have to move because my mom got a new job. I'm going to miss you too," said Reggie. "Who will help me practice my pitching and catching in baseball?! I'll never find another friend like you!" Reggie cried as he hugged Tyson. Tyson returned Reggie's hug and told him that God would help him find another great friend just like him. "And we will still visit each other in the Summer holidays and help each other get better at a bunch of sports," said Tyson. Reggie's mom came into their backyard and told the boys how important it was to speak positively about their lives just like Tyson did. "Gracious words are sweet to the soul and they can even heal you," said his mom. "You and Tyson will stay close. We are praying for you." "Let's pray together right now, okay mom?" asked Reggie. Mom smiled and took the boy's hands. She prayed that Reggie and Tyson would make Godly friends that were new and that they would continue thinking positively about themselves throughout the changes around them. You too can think positively about yourself when you go through hard times. Remember that God is always with you wherever you go.

WEEKLY PRAYER

Dear God, please help me to learn to speak positively about myself instead of speaking negatively about myself. I want to experience peace, joy and love that all come from you, no matter what is going on around me or any changes that take place. Thank you for my life and that nothing catches you by surprise, I trust you to lead me through uncertain times. Amen.

MY PRAYER

THINK GOOD THOUGHTS

"Finally, brothers and sisters, whatever is true, whatever is noble, whatever is right, whatever is pure, whatever is lovely, whatever is admirable - if anything is excellent or praiseworthy - think about such things." Philippians 4:8 NIV

"Why is history so hard?" asked Joey. "It's only facts from the past. Who cares about the past? How am I ever going to pass this test?" His dad came into his room and told him that it was very important to learn about the past because it could teach him a lot about the future. He also mentioned that it was important to think good, positive thoughts. "What do you mean to think good thoughts?" Joey asked. "Well instead of thinking you won't ever understand history before your test, you can think good thoughts about the truth that God tells you. He wants you to think that you will pass the test. He also wants you to think about anything true, noble, right, pure, lovely, admirable, excellent, and praiseworthy," said his dad. "Whenever you think about things in that way you will be able to think good thoughts about yourself more every day. What is your favorite thing about history?" asked his dad. "The fact that we got freedom in 1776," said Joey. "That's something that is excellent and you can even praise God for the freedom we have," said his dad. Joey started to pray that God would help him understand history and help him pass the test. He thanked his dad for his Godly wisdom. On the day of the history test, he asked God to help him remember the important facts. You too can think positively and think good thoughts whenever you have a test to take in school.

WEEKLY PRAYER

Dear God, please help me to think positively and to think about things that are noble, right, excellent, pure, admirable and praiseworthy. Thank you for helping me think good thoughts every day. I want to come to you more when I don't know the reasons for certain things and maybe you can help me understand them by giving me Godly wisdom. Amen.

MY PRAYER

WEEK 28

BRINGING IT TO COMPLETION

"Being confident of this, that he who began a good work in you will carry it on to completion until the day of Christ Jesus."
Philippians 1:8 NIV

Luke couldn't stop coughing. All he wanted to do was go play hockey outside with his friends but he didn't want to get anyone else sick. His mom came into his room to take his temperature and saw that it was still very high. Luke was so exhausted just from coughing and lying in bed. "I'm sorry Luke, but you can't play outside with your friends until your fever goes away," said his mom. "But mom, I was supposed to be the team captain and my teammates are counting on me!" Luke said. "The team knows you're sick, Luke. If your cough doesn't get better in the next two days we will have to go to the doctor," replied his mom. Two days later he was in the doctor's office being diagnosed with pneumonia. "There goes my season of playing hockey!" Luke said frustrated. The doctor sat beside him and tried to encourage him. "Just because you can't play hockey right now, doesn't mean that you'll never play hockey again. Whatever God wants you to do in your life, He will bring it to completion until Jesus comes again," said Doctor Williams. He told Luke to take medicine twice a day for two weeks and he would feel better. Luke believed that he could play hockey again and he also believed that God would help lead his team to more wins during the season. He knew You too can be confident of the plan God has for your life and that He will bring it to completion.

WEEKLY PRAYER

Dear God, please help bring the great work you started in my life to completion. Help me to believe that you will help me accomplish my dreams. Sometimes I doubt your plans in my life when I don't see them happening straight away. I want to have faith that you are in control of my life and trust you with all of my days. Amen.

MY PRAYER

WORKING OUT

"The wise prevail through great power, and those who have knowledge muster their strength." Proverbs 24:5 NIV

Xavier loved working out and running track. He enjoyed the thrill of jumping over hurdles and racing against other competitors. As he got ready for the next track meet, he shouted, "I'm number one! I'm going to win." Coach Henry came up behind him and put his arm around his shoulder. "Xavier, remember what we talked about yesterday during practice? When you have the knowledge about how to compete correctly in sports, you will keep your strength in check," he said. Xavier explained how important track was to him and that he just wanted to win so much and was confident he would. "Feeling good about your abilities starts with being thankful to God for them. Don't brag or boast about how good of an athlete you are because you didn't get your strength and speed just from working out every week. You got your gifts, your health and your talents from God," said Coach Henry. Xavier remembered what his coach told him at the next track meet and thanked God for giving him the wisdom to control his strength. He placed second overall at the track meet. You too can prevail through different sports. God will help you know how to not only control your strength but be thankful for your abilities in every sport you play.

WEEKLY PRAYER

Dear God, please help me to get stronger mentally, physically, emotionally and spiritually. I don't want to rely on my own gifts and talents, but I want to be thankful for all you have blessed me with. I rely on you to protect me and tc keep me healthy but also to grow me into the man you want me to become. Amen.

MY PRAYER

WEEK 30

POWERFUL PRAYERS

"Therefore I tell you, whatever you ask for in prayer, believe that you have received it, and it will be yours." Mark 11:24 NIV

Jordan cried when he heard the news that his grandma had gotten into a car accident, broke her neck and had to be moved to an assisted living facility. "How can this be happening to grandma and our family?" he thought. As his dad called people in his family to pray for Jordan's grandma, he knew he had to pray for her too even though his faith was seriously shaken up. He called the pastor at his church, Pastor Grant and asked him to pray for and over his entire family as they tried to understand how life would be different with his grandmas now living in an assisted facility. "What if God doesn't help heal my grandma?" asked Jordan. Pastor Grant explained that he knew how Jordan was feeling but he encouraged him not to lose his faith even though it was difficult. "Do you remember the message I preached about believing that whatever you ask for in prayer, believe that you will receive it and it will be yours?" he asked. "Yeah. I definitely need to believe that grandma's neck will be healed," said Jordan. They then prayed together. "Lord, you know what Jordan's grandma needs. Please heal her completely and please don't let her have any lasting side effects from this accident and neck fracture," Pastor Grant prayed. Two months later his grandma underwent some testing and the results came back that she did not have any lasting effects from the accident. She also was able to get out of her neck brace. You too can believe for any prayer request to be answered just like Jordan did.

WEEKLY PRAYER

Dear God, thank you that I can come to you and trust you with all of my prayers. Some are big and some are small but to you they are all important. I ask for more faith to believe for the things that I am praying for. Thank you for helping me to believe that I've already received what I prayed for. Amen.

MY PRAYER

MAKING GOOD CHOICES

"You shall not steal." Exodus 20:15 NIV

Adam and his younger brother Brad were spending the night at their grandparent's house. Brad saw money sticking out of grandma's purse. "Look Adam, grandma left money in her wallet. It's tempting to just take the money and go spend it at the shops," said Brad. "No, Brad! We can't steal from grandma. She's letting us stay here all week while mom and dad fix up their house," said Adam. Brad rolled his eyes. "Come on Adam. We can pay her back with the money we make cutting grass this summer. I really want to go buy a new cap," said Brad. Adam stopped him and reminded him of the Bible verse their grandpa had just taught them. "It even says in the Bible that we shouldn't steal anything that doesn't belong to us because that would be breaking the commandments," said Adam. Even though he didn't like being told about potentially breaking the commandments, Brad agreed and sat down on the couch. " I guess we should save our own money to buy what we want, we'll make enough money this summer," said Brad. The next time you're tempted to steal money or anything else, you can remember that God tells you that you shouldn't steal.

Prayer: Dear God, please help me to be wise and to make good choices that benefit my life and strengthen my relationship with you. Stealing from others not only hurts them but it hurts you. I want to make you proud in all of my actions, please help me to make decisions that honor you. Amen.

WEEKLY PRAYER

Dear God, please help me to be wise and to make good choices that benefit my life and strengthen my relationship with you. Stealing from others not only hurts them but it hurts you. I want to make you proud in all of my actions, please help me to make decisions that honor you. Amen.

MY PRAYER

WEEK 32

GOOD SOCIAL MEDIA HABITS

"Let us therefore make every effort to do what leads to peace and to mutual edification." Romans 14:19 NIV

Max was playing games on his iPad and then logged into his Facebook page after not being on there for a week. "OK. Let's see what people are talking about online today," he said. He saw that his friends were arguing in a group chat. He saw that as an opportunity to engage in the conversation. The argument was about a girl in their class named Melanie. Max swooped in and commented that Melanie had a big nose. Within minutes many more of his classmates had engaged in the mean conversation about Melanie. All of a sudden, Max's cell phone rang. It was his friend David. "Why are you starting rumors and saying mean things about Melanie? She didn't do anything to you!" he said. " Oh come on David. It's just a harmless group chat," said Max. "If you don't stop the rumor about Melanie, I could tell Coach Davis and he could kick you off the basketball team. One of his biggest rules is to not engage in gossip online," said David. "Why don't you make the effort to live in peace with people at school even if it's online?" He asked. "OK OK. Fine! I'll take the comment down and apologize to Melanie for the things I've said online," said Max. Whenever you're online you can practice good judgment and live at peace with people. You can ask God to help you have good social media habits and to put yourself in other people's shoes. Instead of looking for the faults in others, ask God to give you his heart for them and to see the good in them.

WEEKLY PRAYER

Dear God, give me the grace and love for others to see the best in them. I ask for your peace to fill my life and help to exercise caution whenever I'm speaking about others, even when I am online. Help me to learn how to spread love and be kind throughout all areas of my life. Amen.

MY PRAYER

WEEK 33

IT'S NOT ABOUT YOU

"Don't let anyone look down on you because you are young, but set an example for the believers in speech, in conduct, in love, in faith and in purity." 1 Timothy 4:12 NIV

"Grandpa, how can I tell people about Jesus and everything he has done in my life?" asked Ryan. "I'm only 12 years old, no one will listen to me?" "Did you know that you're never too young to tell others about Jesus?" said grandpa. "It says in the Bible to not let anyone look down on you because you're young. You can set an example for other believers in the way you act, talk and think," said grandpa. "The other important thing to remember is that telling people about God is not about your reputation. Rather, it's about setting an example for other Christians and especially for people who don't know Jesus." Ryan was intrigued by his grandpa's insight and said he wanted to teach people about Jesus right away. He and grandpa prayed that God would help him be brave and spread the gospel to his family and friends. God will help you be brave enough to spread His love to the people around you when you are confident that he lives in you.

WEEKLY PRAYER

Dear God, thank you for allowing me to be an example for others in the things I say and do. Thank you for reminding me that my life is not about what I can do,, but rather about what you can do in me and through me. Give me opportunities to speak to others about how your love has changed my life. I want to represent you in all I do. Amen.

MY PRAYER

GOD KEEPS YOU SAFE

"In peace I will lie down and sleep, for you alone, Lord, make me dwell in safety." Psalm 4:8 NIV

Greg woke up in a cold sweat after having a nightmare about something happening to him and his family while they were on vacation. He went straight to his dad and woke him up. "Did you have another bad dream son?" his dad asked. Greg nodded and asked his dad to give him a hug. "I know you love my hugs because they make you feel safe. But did you know that Jesus hugs you in different ways?" Greg was curious, "Really, how?" His dad explained that Jesus hugs people through the family and friends that he places in their lives and that he also hugs people through His Word. "Jesus doesn't want you to be afraid to sleep at night. He wants you to be able to lay down and sleep in peace because he and the angels are watching over you and Jesus helps you dwell in safety. Do you believe that?" dad asked. Greg smiled, nodded and instantly felt safe. He prayed, "Dear God, please help me to go back to sleep. Thank you for always watching over me." No matter what you're facing, you too can ask God to help you lay down and sleep in peace every night.

WEEKLY PRAYER

Dear God, thank you for always keeping me safe no matter where I go. Thank you for the blessing of laying down at n ght and being able to sleep in peace. I ask for you to protect my dreams and refresh me as I sleep. Amen.

MY PRAYER

SAFELY PLAYING SPORTS

"The name of the Lord is a fortified tower; the righteous run to it and are safe." Proverbs 18:10 NIV

Mitchell loved playing sports but his favorite sport was football. He loved learning about God and football from Coach Walker. "Are you guys ready for the game this weekend?" Asked Coach Walker. The entire team yelled that they were ready and shouted with excitement. "Alright Mitch, you're going to protect the other players, run fast and tackle hard. This team is just like your family. You all protect and love each other. Just like God protects and loves you," said Coach Walker. "The name of the Lord is a strong tower. When you run to Him, you are safe whether you're on the field playing football, at the shops with your friends, or sitting on the bus going to school. God keeps you safe. When we play football, it is the entire team's job to look out for each other and keep each other safe while playing the game." Mitch and the team knew they had to count on each other to play the game and trust God to keep them safe throughout it. You too can count on your teammates and God to help you stay safe when trying to win a football game.

WEEKLY PRAYER

Dear God, Thank you for always being there for me. I ask for your help and your protection over me whenever I am playing sports. Please help me to teach others about trusting you and running to you when they feel like they need your strength. I know I can always depend on you. Amen.

MY PRAYER

WEEK 36

DISCERNMENT

"And this is my prayer: that your love may abound more and more in knowledge and depth of insight, so that you may be able to discern what is best and may be pure and blameless for the day of Christ," Philippians 1: 9-10 NIV

Tucker and his brother Grayson were playing kickball in the backyard with their friends. Without thinking Tucker backed up and ran as fast as he could, kicking the ball with everything he had. The ball sailed through the air and went right into the garage window. The glass broke all over the back patio. "Oh man. You guys are screwed," yelled one of their friends. "See ya! Wouldn't want to be ya," yelled another friend. Tucker and Grayson looked at each other wondering what they could do. "We could lie about who cracked the window and pin it on one of our friends," suggested Grayson. "No! Remember how we learned in our Bible study that we have to be able to discern what to do in every area of our lives?" said Tucker. "Stop being such a perfectionist," said Grayson. "We gotta agree on the same story, right now! Mom could see the garage window any minute," said Tucker. Let's pray about what we should do." They both came to the conclusion that it would be better to tell their parents the truth about how they broke the window playing kickball. Their parents were very pleased that the boys told them the truth, but disappointed that they broke the window. The boys offered up their savings money and also suggested they do various other chores to help pay for the window themselves. You too can learn to discern what is best in your life with God's help.

WEEKLY PRAYER

Dear God, please help me to be truthful and honest in my words and actions. Help me to discern what is best for my life. I want to be able to discern what is right and what is wrong, making you proud of the things I do and who I am. Thank you for seeing me be as pure and blameless even w1en I get it wrong. Amen.

MY PRAYER

TRUSTING IN GOD'S PLAN

"Commit to the Lord whatever you do, and he will establish your plans." Proverbs 16:3 NIV

Joe was scared. He just found out that his mom had been diagnosed with cancer. He didn't want to see his mom being so sick. He just continually gave her his love and support. One day when she was completely bedridden because of her illness, Joe started reading the Bible with her. She admitted her faith was being shaken. One of the verses he read talked about committing everything you do to the Lord and then he would establish your plans. "Is there anything that is stopping you from feeling free?" he asked. "I haven't spoken to your grandma in a whole year. I should patch things up with her," said mom. "I know you haven't talked to grandma in a long time, but I'm sure she would appreciate you making the first move to reconcile the relationship," said Joe. They took each other's hands and prayed that God would give his mom the right words when she tried to talk to grandma. Mom admitted that she was nervous to try and talk to her, but Sam gave her a hug and told her to trust in God's plan for her life. His mom called grandma and the two ended up talking for hours and made up with each other. Mom thanked God for helping them make up. She also thanked Joe for telling her to trust in God's plan. You can trust in God's plan for you and your life. You'll also have opportunities to help others trust God for his plan in theirs.

WEEKLY PRAYER

Dear God, please help me to commit everything I do to you. Thank you for already putting your wonderful plans for my life into motion. I know that sometimes I can't see the outcomes, but you do. Thank you for caring for me and creating such great plans for my life. Amen.

MY PRAYER

HELPING OTHERS KNOW JESUS

"You are my witnesses," declares the Lord," Isaiah 43:10 NIV

Liam was watching a football game on TV with his friend Noah. "Do you know Jesus?" asked Liam. "Who's Jesus?" replied Noah. Liam smiled and realized that it was the perfect opportunity to tell Noah about Jesus. Liam explained to Noah that God loved us so much that He sent Jesus to die on the cross to save everyone from their sins. Liam also explained that Jesus loved Noah even more than his family ever could. "Jesus sounds incredible," said Noah. "How do I get to know Him?" "All you have to do is ask Jesus to come into your heart and forgive you of your sins," said Liam. Noah asked Liam to pray with him so he could receive Jesus in his life. "Hey Lord," Liam began. "My friend Noah really wants to know you and have a personal relationship with you." Noah prayed that Jesus would come into his heart and forgive him of all of his sins. "Please help me to know you, Lord," said Noah. Later that year, Liam asked Noah if he wanted to go on a teenage mission trip with him and his church youth group. Noah happily agreed and went along. "I can't wait to tell other people about Jesus, just like you told me about Jesus," said Noah. You too, can be excited to tell your friends and family about Jesus and how much he loves them when the opportunities arise.

WEEKLY PRAYER

Dear God, please help me to share your love and mercy with everyone I meet. I want to be bold and brave in my faith and never miss an opportunity that you give me to share about how great you are. Thank you for the privilege to witness and tell others about you, every day. Amen.

MY PRAYER

YOU DON'T HAVE BECAUSE YOU DON'T ASK

"Until now you have not asked for anything in my name. Ask and you will receive, and your joy will be complete." John 16:24 NIV

Jayden really wanted to go to the arcade to play some games with his friends. He started to make plans to sneak out of the house and go to the arcade. As he was running out of the house, his mom spotted him. "Where are you off to?" she asked. Jayden didn't want to tell her that he was going to the arcade so he tried to be cool about it. "I'm going to the library to study with my friend Ray," he said. "You never run out of the house like that to study with anyone," said mom. "Where were you really going?" "Ok. I really wanted to go to the arcade to play some air hockey but I figured that you and dad wouldn't let me go because it's a school night," he said. "You automatically assumed that we wouldn't let you go to the arcade? But you will never get the answers to anything unless you ask. So, ask me," said mom. Jayden was silent for a moment, thinking about what his mom had just said. "Can I please go play air hockey?" Jayden asked. "Jayden, you did so very well on your last report card. You can go today, but be home by 6 p.m.," said mom. Jayden smiled and ran to hug her while telling her thank you. "Jayden, you never need to lie to me, I will always trust you to make good decisions when you are honest with me," said mom. Whenever you think your parents won't let you go somewhere, don't just assume that they won't. Be brave enough to ask them and see what they say. Being honest and communicating openly with your parents can help strengthen your relationship with them and also honors God in the process. You can also ask God for anything, he did create the heavens and the earth.

WEEKLY PRAYER

Dear God, I don't want to be afraid to ask you for anything. Help me to be bold in my prayers and believe that I'll receive what I ask for. You have given me a heart that knows how to be honest and truthful, help me to choose what makes you proud every day. Thank you for filling me with joy. Give me opportunities to help others see the joy you have placed in their lives too. Amen.

MY PRAYER

WEEK 40

BE CONFIDENT IN WHAT YOU DON'T SEE

"Now faith is confidence in what we hope for and assurance about what we do not see." Hebrews 11:1 NIV

Phillip felt like his world had just turned upside down. His grandpa had just been diagnosed with a virus that the doctors weren't sure they could heal. "Mom, what do I do? I don't want anything bad to happen to grandpa!" said Phillip. "You have to keep trusting God and keep your faith, trust that grandpa will be healed in Jesus' name. Remember what Pastor Aaron said? Having faith is having confidence in what we hope for and assurance about what we don't see," said mom. Every day he and his mom prayed for his grandpa to be healed. After more than a month, Phillip became discouraged that his prayers weren't being answered fast enough. "Don't give up on praying for grandpa, buddy. Just because you don't see something happening doesn't mean that Jesus isn't working on grandpa's behalf. Jesus hears all of your prayers whether they're big or small. He hears everything you pray for grandpa even when you haven't said it out loud. Even though you may not see his physical healing, God is still healing grandpa from the inside out. After another month, his grandpa's strength started to return, little by little. Grandpa started to participate in family cookouts and started going to Phillip's baseball games. He thanked Phillip for never giving up on him and for praying for his complete healing. Whenever someone you know gets sick, continually ask God for their healing and believe with the faith you have that they will be healed. Even though you may not see the miracle of healing right away, believe that it will happen.

WEEKLY PRAYER

Dear God, please help me to place my confidence in you even when I don't see you or feel you. I don't want to doubt what you can do, so give me the faith to believe for others, and even myself. Please give me your blessed assurance throughout my life. Amen.

MY PRAYER

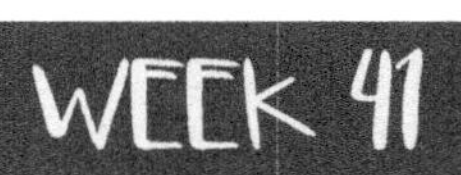

NEVER GIVE UP

"Let us not become weary in doing good, for at the proper time we will reap a harvest if we do not give up." Galatians 6:9 NIV

Logan went into the kitchen to do the dishes before his mom got home from work. "Can I help you dry the dishes?" asked his younger brother Isaac. "Sure," said Logan. Isaac asked why it was so important to do the dishes right away instead of leaving them until the last minute. Logan explained that it was important because then they would have time to do what they wanted to do later on, like, ride their bikes. "It is also important to do the chores mom asked us to do before we forget about them. God can help us not grow weary in doing good, even if we don't feel like doing the dishes because if we don't give up we will be blessed. Also, any time I do help around the house, I think of it as if I am serving the Lord," said Logan. "So, God will help us to want to do our chores and feel good about them?" asked Isaac. Logan handed him a plate to dry and suggested they dust and vacuum the living room also before mom got home. Isaac agreed and went to get the vacuum. He finished vacuuming and dusting while Logan finished the dishes. When mom arrived home, she saw how nice the house looked and praised the boys for their efforts. God is glad when you don't give up on doing good for others whether you do the dishes, vacuum, dust, or do any of your chores.

WEEKLY PRAYER

Dear God, I never want to give up on doing good for others. Thank you for helping me remain strong and consistent in helping, serving and doing good for others. Life can get hard but I trust you in any challenges that I encounter to bring the fruit out. Amen.

MY PRAYER

LOVE YOUR NEIGHBOR

"You have heard that it was said, 'Love your neighbor and hate your enemy.' But I tell you, love your enemies and pray for those who persecute you," Matthew 5:43-44 NIV

Oliver couldn't take it anymore. He was constantly being bullied at school. He went into his next class crying. His teacher Mrs. Wallace saw him sitting at his desk before the class began and asked him what was wrong. "Kids were saying really mean things about me. I really want to hurt them the way they hurt me. They were saying that I won't pass sixth grade, because I'm struggling with three subjects," said Oliver. Mrs. Wallace said she would talk to the entire class about being nicer to each other. Ten minutes later she started the lesson. "Can anyone read the Bible verse of the day for us?" she asked. Oliver raised his hand bravely and read the Bible verse. Mrs. Wallace continued explaining that none of the students should make fun of, bully or hurt their other classmates. "Even though you might want to get even with the students who have hurt you, God wants you to love them and pray for them," she said. She silently prayed that this Bible verse and this thought got through to Oliver's bullies. Later that day she saw Oliver talking to the boys who bullied him. Instead of fighting and arguing, the boys were talking and laughing. "I know I'll be able to pass my classes," said Oliver, " I hope you're able to pass your classes too." He felt good about being nice to them instead of being mean and knew God would be proud of him for this.

WEEKLY PRAYER

Dear God, please help me to love those that hurt me and have a soft heart. I don't want to be bitter to those who have bullied me. Please help me to extend grace to the people who hurt me, let resilience rise up in me that I can lean on to remain steadfast and strong in you. Amen.

MY PRAYER

WEEK 43

YOUR FIRST CRUSH

"I can do all this through him who gives me strength,"
Philippians 4:13 NIV

Gabriel had started to develop a crush on a girl in his class named Connie. Every time he saw her he felt butterflies in his stomach, but he wasn't sure how he could talk to her. He decided to ask his grandpa about it. "Just be yourself. Ask her if she wants to hang out after school. You're both on the soccer team aren't you?" grandpa asked. Gabriel nodded. "What do I say?" he asked. Grandpa explained that Gabriel could ask her for help with running and passing the soccer ball and that would give them an excuse to hang out more together. The next day Gabriel saw Connie running across the field. She scored a goal and waved to Gabriel. As they finished soccer practice, Gabriel asked Connie if she wouldn't mind helping him pass the ball better. "Sure," she said. As everyone left the field they stayed behind and practiced. "All you have to do is keep your eye on the ball and move your feet fast enough so no one can take it from you," she said. As Gabriel tried racing down the field, Connie intercepted the ball. "See? You have to be faster and move your feet to be behind the ball and control it. You can do all things through Christ who gives you strength," said Connie. Gabriel's heart was racing but found confidence in himself and the friendship he was forming with Connie. Over the next few weeks, they continued practicing soccer together and Gabriel was able to score two goals in the next game. He kept repeating Philippians 4:13 before and during every game and it gave him more confidence and was thankful to Connie for the coaching she had given him and the friendship they were growing.

WEEKLY PRAYER

Dear God, please help me to remember that I can do all things through you who gives me strength. Life is tough at times but I know that if I hold on to this verse, I can always find strength to do things that make me nervous. I want to be strong because I represent you. Amen.

MY PRAYER

HOW YOU CAN FORGIVE

"And when you stand praying, if you hold anything against anyone, forgive them, so that your Father in heaven may forgive you your sins." Mark 11:25 NIV

Sebastian was angry at his older brother Sean for always hogging the TV and playing video games when he got home. He asked him nicely multiple times to let him have a turn on the play station. "No! I'm not letting you have a turn. You had the play station all weekend," said Sean. Sebastian didn't feel like forgiving him for not sharing the game. "Do you remember the verse grandpa told us when we stayed over at their house?" asked Sean. "Don't preach to me now," said Sebastian. Dad walked into the living room and told them to stop arguing with each other. "The last time you did something mean to Sean, he forgave you. Now it's your turn to forgive him, Sebastian," said dad. Jesus said when you're praying, if you hold anything against someone forgive them so God may forgive you. I'm guessing both of you want to be forgiven for the sins you commit?" he asked. The boys looked at their father and then at each other. "I forgive you for not sharing the game with me," said Sebastian. "Thank you. Maybe we can each have 30 minutes each on the play station every day and share it fairly?" said Sean. Sebastian agreed and they split the time on the play station. They also thanked their dad for his wisdom. You can forgive your siblings just like God forgives you.

WEEKLY PRAYER

Dear God, please help me to be willing to forgive others just like you're willing to forgive me. I don't want to hold any unforgiveness in my heart towards those I care about. Help me to keep my eyes on you and what you would do when I face unforgiveness and holding grudges. Amen.

MY PRAYER

GODLY GUIDANCE

"Start children off on the way they should go, and even when they are old they will not turn from it." Proverbs 22:6 NIV

Wyatt couldn't wait to get home to practice basketball. As soon as he got home, he set his backpack down and went to the backyard to play even though he knew he had homework to finish. A few minutes later his mom came out into the yard telling him that he had to finish his homework before he played basketball. "Ah mom, come on! Just let me practice for an hour and then I'll finish my homework," said Wyatt. "No, you have to finish your homework now. Even though you don't want to, you have to start putting your work before your play. It's important because it teaches you about your priorities and it helps you feel even more accomplished when you focus on your work and finish it before switching off," said mom. She continued explaining how she wanted to train him in the way he should do things, just as the Bible says. "The earlier I teach you to put your work before play, the easier it will be for you to understand that priorities are important," said mom. Wyatt reluctantly went to finish his homework before he returned outside to play basketball. He felt accomplished as he finished his homework and went to play. You too can receive Godly guidance in your life even if finishing your homework isn't what you want to do right now, finishing it on time will help you feel more accomplished and disciplined.

WEEKLY PRAYER

Dear God, I want to honor you by remaining disciplined and organized. Please help me to seek out Godly guidance from my family and friends. I pray that each day I can learn how to act in a way that's pleasing to you and glorifies you. Amen.

MY PRAYER

DREAM BIG

"Now to him who is able to do immeasurably more than all we ask or imagine, according to his power that is at work within us,"
Romans 3:20 NIV

Zachary was dreaming about his future career. He wanted to be a marine biologist and study animals in the ocean. Ever since his parents had taken him to the ocean for the first time when he was five years old, he had been fascinated with the ocean, but also been afraid of its power. His friend Harry said it could be challenging to become a marine biologist because of his fear of water. "Even though you're afraid of the ocean, there are plenty of other things that you can do as a career," said Harry. Zachary thought about it. "Maybe I'll be a music instructor. But that seems like a small dream compared to becoming a marine biologist," he thought. Zachary reminded himself to put his dreams in God's hands whether they seemed big or small. He remembered the scripture, "God can do more than we can ask of, think of, and even more than we can imagine." Zachary was encouraged as he thought about this scripture and knew that with God anything was impossible, even becoming a marine biologist. You have your whole life to dream big dreams and accomplish your goals. Even when you have dreams that seem unattainable, God can help you accomplish them. Never give up on the dreams that God has placed in your heart.

WEEKLY PRAYER

Dear God, I believe that you will be able to help me accomplish anything that I dream. Please give me courage to dream big throughout my life. Thank you that you're able to do more in my life than I can ever imagine and I trust you completely. Amen.

MY PRAYER

WEEK 47

ENJOYING EVERYDAY LIFE

"A person can do nothing better than to eat and drink and find satisfaction in their own toil. This too, I see, is from the hand of God," Ecclesiastes 2:24 NIV

Greg loved playing with his Frisbee. He loved playing it so much that he started to forget about doing his homework. "Greg, it's time to start your homework," said dad. "No!" I just want to keep playing Frisbee and I'll do my homework later," said Greg. "Besides, doesn't it say in the Bible to eat, drink and be happy?" His dad explained that the Bible did say that people should always enjoy themselves but he also told him that it was very important to do his homework so he could learn more, be more confident at school and become smarter. "If you do your homework first, you will have more time for playing with your Frisbee," said dad. "OK I'll make time for my homework first from now on," Greg said. He thanked God for allowing him to learn and for his talents to throw and catch a Frisbee. You can enjoy yourself and make sure you prioritize your schoolwork at the same time.

WEEKLY PRAYER

Dear God, I want you to be the center of my life. Please help me to enjoy my life but also understand the importance of learning and doing school work. Help me to see the joy in everyday life, you have created me to enjoy it. Thank you for all you have blessed me with. Amen.

MY PRAYER

HELPING THOSE IN NEED

"Whoever is kind to the poor lends to the Lord, and he will reward them for what they have done." Proverbs 19:17 NIV

Austin loved volunteering at his church. He really wanted to go on a mission trip to Africa that his church was organizing. His parents knew how important spreading the gospel was to Austin, and they helped cover the cost of the mission trip. When Austin got to Africa, a bunch of small children ran to him and surrounded him, giving him hugs. He noticed that a lot of the kids didn't have shoes. He asked his youth leader Mr. Brown how he could help those kids. "We bought shoes and toys for the kids. You can help us distribute them tomorrow," Mr. Arnold said. Austin smiled and said he couldn't wait. The next morning he started handing out shoes and toys. The childrens' faces lit up and they couldn't believe that someone cared enough to give them shoes. With the help of a translator, Austin was able to tell the kids about Jesus and how they could have a personal relationship with Him. Whenever you see people who are less fortunate than you, you can be a blessing to them whether you give them shoes, toys or share the message of Jesus with them.

WEEKLY PRAYER

Dear God, I want to make a difference in this world so teach me how I can help. I specifically want to help the people in my life that are in need. Show me different ways to help the poor and needy in my community and around the world. Amen.

MY PRAYER

BELIEVE IN YOURSELF

"Truly I tell you, if you have faith as small as a mustard seed, you can say to this mountain, 'Move from here to there,' and it will move. Nothing will be impossible for you." Matthew 17:20 NIV

Archie was doubting that he could get over his fear of swimming. "What about swimming scares you?" asked his brother Kenny. "Opening my eyes and holding my breath underwater, and what if I swim crooked instead of swimming straight? But also jumping off the high dive!" answered Archie. "I have to jump off the high dive and swim in the 13-foot-deep water if I want to become a lifeguard later in my life." Kenny explained to Archie that he should pray about all of the things he was scared to do in the pool. "You have to believe in yourself and say that you can get over your fears little by little. If you have faith as small as a mustard seed you can move a mountain and nothing will be impossible for you," said Kenny. The next time Archie went to his swim lesson, he remembered what Kenny said. He told himself, " I know I can swim well and am brave enough to jump off the diving board with God's help." You too can believe in yourself and your abilities. Nothing will be impossible for you when you have faith in God.

WEEKLY PRAYER

Dear God, I am so sure of you that my faith is so important to me. Please help me to believe in myself in the same way that you believe in me. I ask for you to increase my faith and I trust that you will guide me through each and every day. Amen.

MY PRAYER

WALKING IN FAITH

"Consequently, faith comes from hearing the message, and the message is heard through the word about Christ."
Romans 10:17 NIV

Brian was excited about giving his speech at school. He was going to tell people how important a relationship with Jesus was. When it was his turn to speak, he took a deep breath, said a quick prayer and trusted that God would give him the right words. "Who is your truest friend?" he asked the class. Some students said their siblings, their cousins, and their classmates. "Did you know that your truest friend can be God?" he continued to explain that they could get to know God by asking Him into their hearts, by reading God's word every day, and by going to church every week. "When you hear His message, you learn more about Him. When you learn more about Him, you'll trust Him more. Walking in faith means trusting in God even if you don't understand His plan," said Brian. He continued telling the class that his goal in life was to spread the gospel around the school and in his community. "Walking in faith doesn't mean that everyone will accept your message, but people can get to know Christ through your words and actions," said Brian. Your faith will grow every time you hear God's word. You can reach out to the people in your life and walk in faith every day.

WEEKLY PRAYER

Dear God, help me to walk in faith with you every day. Help me to hear and understand your message. I want to take every opportunity to share my faith with others and I ask for you to help make this happen daily. Amen

MY PRAYER

GRATEFUL

"Always giving thanks to God the Father for everything, in the name of our Lord Jesus Christ." Ephesians 5:20 NIV

"Stop taking my stuff!" Kevin yelled at his younger brother Jack. "Grandma gave me the new scooter for my birthday! It doesn't mean you can use it!" Instead of listening to him, Jack zoomed down their driveway on Kevin's scooter. "Dad! Jack keeps using my scooter even though I told him not to," Kevin complained. Before dad could tell Jack to give Kevin back his scooter, a car came out of nowhere hitting him and knocking him to the ground. The thoughts of the scooter went out of Kevin's mind. He and his dad rushed to Jack's side as he moaned in pain on the ground. Their dad called 9-1-1 and the EMTs rushed to the scene. Kevin felt guilty for telling Jack that he couldn't use his scooter. "Dad, all I want is for Jack to be ok," said Kevin. They joined hands at the hospital and prayed that Jack would be ok with no lasting injuries. The doctor came out an hour later and told them that Jack's only injury was a broken arm. Dad and Kevin hugged, grateful that Jack would be ok. When Kevin entered Jack's hospital room he gave him a huge hug. "I'm so grateful you're my brother, and I'm so grateful you're ok" he said. "You can use my scooter any time, but first your arm has to heal!" Kevin said kindly. God can use difficult circumstances to help you be grateful for the family he gave you.

WEEKLY PRAYER

Dear God, thank you for my family. Please help me to always be grateful for my siblings and to value them over anything I own. You have placed us in the same family, so let us encourage each other and work as a team. Amen.

MY PRAYER

EXTEND GRACE

"But to each one of us grace has been given as Christ apportioned it." Ephesians 4:7 NIV

"Dane, it's time for dinner," yelled his brother Conner. As he sat down at the kitchen table, Dane started to complain. "Ew! Meatloaf for dinner?!" he complained. "Seriously? You couldn't make something better?" Conner sighed loudly and told him that he made dinner because their parents were both working overnight shifts. Instead of getting mad at him for complaining about the meal, he extended grace to his little brother. "The least you could do is say thank you! I know the dinner may not be what we both want, but I had to make something simple. The next time we can make it together. How about that?" He asked. Dane smiled at him. "Really? You want to cook with me even after I complained about the meatloaf? Why?" he asked, shocked. "I've been reading the Bible and it says that every one of us has been given grace by Jesus Christ," said Conner. "So I have to extend grace to you, mom, dad and anyone else I meet. Jesus extended grace to me so how can I not extend grace to you even though we drive each other crazy at times?" Conner said smiling. The two brothers laughed and began eating their dinner. You too can offer up grace to anyone who might annoy you or drive you crazy.

WEEKLY PRAYER

Dear God, you have been so kind to me and I am so thankful for your grace in and over my life. Please help me to extend grace and mercy to everyone around me, in the same way that you've shown it to me. Let people know that I belong to you because of my love and grace for them. Amen

MY PRAYER

CONCLUSION

No matter what circumstances you face in your life God sees you, hears the cries from the depths of your heart and wants what is best for you. You are His precious daughter, His beloved child and He cares for you. No matter what you are feeling, take it to Him and ask Jesus to help you through it. No matter what happens, He is always with you and He will never let you down. He has the best plans in store for your life and they are better than you could ever imagine. Trust that even though you don't see a way through a situation, Jesus has already won the battle by dying in your place on the cross. Trust that God will see you through to the other side. He will give you His victory. Keep your eyes, ears and heart focused on Him every day and you will get through anything that comes your way. God will make a way when there seems to be no way and He will help you bring others to know Him through your words and actions. Remember, just because you are young, doesn't mean you can't make a difference for the Kingdom of God. Treating others like Jesus would treat them can make a big impact on someone's life and it will show them the love of God inside you. You're never too young to talk about your faith and how Jesus has impacted and changed your life. I pray that this devotional encouraged you throughout the year and that you gained new insight into how to walk closely with Jesus every week.

GLOSSARY

Priority: Treating a task as very important

Casting: Putting something out, away from you, letting something go like casting a net while fishing

Peaceful: Free from disturbance, calm, relaxed

Corrupting talk: Acting dishonestly for personal gain, saying mean things to someone else

Worry: Excessive thoughts of bad things that may or may not happen, allowing yourself to think about trials/problems

Encourage: Build one another up

Completion: Finishing a task

Temple: A beautiful place where people go to worship. Treating your body like a temple means honoring it by eating, doing, and saying the right things.

Pure: Blameless, clean, free of any illness or germs

Obey: Do what someone asks of you. Do what someone tells you to do, happily or even when you don't want to.

Confidence: Fully relying on someone or something. Believing fully in God.

Secret: Something you or a friend tell one another and don't tell anyone else. Something private.

Lamp: A bright light

Grace: Being nice to people who may or may not deserve it.

Transformed: Making a dramatic change

Combat: Taking action to prevent or reduce something

Discernment: The ability to judge well, knowing the difference between right and wrong, good and bad

Guard: Watch over in order to protect

Dwell: Be in/live in a specified place

Workmanship: The skill by which a job is done/ God's perfect work in your life

REFERENCES

Scripture quotations, unless otherwise noted, are taken from the Holy Bible via the following sources: Holy Bible, New International Version®, NIV® Copyright ©1973, 1978, 1984, 2011 by Biblica, Inc.®
Mark 11:24 (NIV) "Therefore I tell you, whatever you ask for in prayer, believe that you have received it, and it will be yours."

1 Peter 5:7 (NIV) "Cast all your anxiety on Him because he cares for you."

Philippians 4:13 (NIV) "I can do all this through him who gives me strength."

John 10:10 (NIV) "I have come that they may have life, and have it to the full."

Mathew 7:7 (NIV) "Ask and it will be given to you; seek and you will find; knock and the door will be opened to you."

Romans 12:18 (NIV) "If it is possible so far as it depends on you live peacefully with everyone"

Ephesians 4:29 (NIV) "Do not let any unwholesome talk come out of your mouths, but only what is helpful for building others up according to their needs, that it may benefit those who listen."

John 14:27 (NIV) "Peace I leave with you; my peace I give you. I do not give to you as the world gives. "Do not let your hearts be troubled and do not be afraid."

Mathew 6:34 (NIV) "Therefore do not worry about tomorrow, for tomorrow will worry about itself. "Each day has enough trouble of its own."

Psalm 139: 14 NIV "I praise you because I am fearfully and wonderfully made; your works are wonderful; I know that full well"

Mathew 6:37 NIV

1 Thessalonians 5:11 (NIV) "Therefore encourage one another and build each other up, just as in fact you are doing."

1 John 4:4 (NIV) "You, dear children, are from God and have overcome them, because the one who is in you is greater than the one who is in the world."

Philippians 1:6 (NIV) "Being confident of this, that he who began a good work in you will carry it on to completion until the day of Christ Jesus"

Jude 1:20 (NIV) "But you, dear friends, by building yourselves up in your most holy faith and praying in the Holy Spirit"

1 Corinthians 6:19-20 (NIV) "Do you not know that your bodies are temples of the Holy Spirit, who is in you, whom you have received from God? You are not your own; you were bought at a price. Therefore honor God with your bodies."

16. Mathew 5:8 (NIV) "Blessed are the pure in heart, for they will see God."

17. 1 Thesalonians 5:17 (NIV) "Pray without ceasing"

18. Ephesians 5:20 (NIV) "Always giving thanks to God the Father for everything, in the name of our Lord Jesus Christ."

19. Proverbs 27:10 (NIV) "Do not forsake your friend or a friend of your family"

20. Deuteronomy 5:16 (NIV) "Honor your father and your mother, as the Lord your God has commanded you, so that you may live long and that it may go well with you in the land the Lord your God is giving you."

21. John 14:27 {NIV) My command is this: Love each other as I have loved you."

22. Mathew 28:19 NIV "Therefore go and make disciples of all nations, baptizing them in the name of the Father and of the Son and of the Holy Spirit."

22. Hebrews 11:1 (NIV) "Now faith is confidence in what we hope for and assurance about what we do not see."

23. Ephesians 6:18 (NIV) "And pray in the Spirit on all occasions with all kinds of prayers and requests. With this in mind, be alert and always keep on praying for all the Lord's people."

24. John 3:16 (NIV) "For God so loved the world that he gave his one and only Son, that whoever believes in him shall not perish but have eternal life."

25.Exodus 20:12 (NIV) "Honor your father and your mother, so that you may live long in the land the Lord your God is giving you."

26. Mathew 6:6 (NIV) "But when you pray, go into your room, close the

door and pray to your Father, who is unseen. Then your Father, who sees what is done in secret, will reward you."

27. Psalm 119:105 (NIV) "Your word is a lamp for my feet, a light on my path."

28. Philippians 2:3 (NIV) "Do nothing out of selfish ambition or vain conceit. Rather, in humility value others above yourselves"

29. 2 Corinthians 9:8 (NIV) "And God is able to bless you abundantly, so that in all things at all times, having all that you need, you will abound in every good work."

30. Hebrews 13:6 (NIV) "So we say with confidence, The Lord is my helper; I will not be afraid. What can mere mortals do to me?"

31. Romans 12:2 (NIV) "Be transformed by the renewing of your mind. Then you will be able to test and approve what God's will is—His good, pleasing and perfect will"

32. Amos 5:4 (NIV) "This is what the Lord says to Israel: Seek me and live"

33. Mathew 6:1 (NIV) "Be careful not to practice your righteousness in front of others to be seen by them. If you do, you will have no reward from your Father in heaven."

34. James 3:17 (NIV) "But the wisdom that comes from heaven is first of all pure; then peace-loving, considerate, submissive, full of mercy and good fruit, impartial and sincere."

35. 2 Timothy 1:7 (NIV) "For the Spirit God gave us does not make us timid, but gives us power, love and self-discipline."

36. Philippians 1:9-10 (NIV) "And this is my prayer: that your love may abound more and more in knowledge and depth of insight, so that you may be able to discern what is best"

37. 2 Corinthians 12:9 (NIV) "But he said to me, My grace is sufficient for you, for my power is made perfect in weakness. Therefore I will boast all the more gladly about my weaknesses, so that Christ's power may rest on me."

38. Psalm 141:3 (NIV) "Set a guard over my mouth, Lord; keep watch over the door of my lips."

39. Jeremiah 29:11 (NIV) "For I know the plans I have for you," declares

the Lord, "plans to prosper you and not to harm you, plans to give you hope and a future."

40. Romans 8:26 (NIV) "In the same way, the Spirit helps us in our weakness. We do not know what we ought to pray for, but the Spirit himself intercedes for us through wordless groans."

41. Proverbs 17:17 (NIV) "A friend loves at all times, and a brother is born for a time of adversity."

42. Mathew 18:20 (NIV) "For where two or three gather in my name, there am I with them."

43. Psalm 4:8 (NIV) "In peace I will lie down and sleep, for you alone, Lord, make me dwell in safety."

44. James 5:16 (NIV) "The prayer of a righteous person is powerful and effective."

45. Philippians 3:12 (NIV) Not that I have already obtained all this, or have already arrived at my goal, but I press on to take hold of that for which Christ Jesus took hold of me.

46. Philippians 3:14 (NIV) "I press on toward the goal to win the prize for which God has called me heavenward in Christ Jesus."

47. Mathew 6:37 (NIV) "Who by worrying can add a single hour to your life?"

48. Psalm 31:30 NIV "Charm is deceptive, and beauty is fleeting, but a woman who fears the Lord is to be praised"

49. Ephesians 2:10 (NIV) "For we are God's handiwork, created in Christ Jesus to do good works, which God prepared in advance for us to do."

50. Proverbs 31:25 (NIV) "She is clothed with strength and dignity; she can laugh at the days to come."

51. 3 John 1:2 (NIV) "Dear friend, I pray that you may enjoy good health and that all may go well with you, even as your soul is getting along well."

52. John 15:12 (NIV) "My command is this: Love each other as I have loved you. "

Made in the USA
Las Vegas, NV
02 January 2024

83774435R00066